QUICK
AND EASY
COOKING

QUICK
AND EASY
COOKING

Grange
BOOKS

Published by Grange Books
An imprint of Books & Toys Limited
The Grange
Grange Yard
London SE1 3AG
By arrangement with Ebury Press

ISBN 1 85627 122 6

Consultant editor: Jeni Wright
Editors: Veronica Sperling and Barbara Croxford
Design: Mike Leaman
Illustrations: John Woodcock and Kate Simunek
Photography: David Johnson
Cookery: Susanna Tee, Maxine Clark, Janet Smith

Filmset by Advanced Filmsetters (Glasgow) Ltd

Printed and bound in Italy by
New Interlitho, S.p.a., Milan

CONTENTS

COOKERY NOTES

Follow either metric or imperial measures for the recipes in this book as they are not inter-changeable. Sets of spoon measures are available in both metric and imperial size to give accurate measurement of small quantities. All spoon measures are level unless otherwise stated. When measuring milk we have used the exact conversion of 568 ml (1 pint).

* Size 4 eggs should be used except when otherwise stated.

† Granulated sugar is used un-less otherwise stated.

● Plain flour is used unless otherwise stated.

OVEN TEMPERATURE CHART

°C	°F	Gas mark
110	225	$\frac{1}{4}$
130	250	$\frac{1}{2}$
140	275	1
150	300	2
170	325	3
180	350	4
190	375	5
200	400	6
220	425	7
230	450	8
240	475	9

METRIC CONVERSION SCALE

LIQUID			SOLID		
Imperial	*Exact conversion*	*Recommended ml*	*Imperial*	*Exact conversion*	*Recommended g*
$\frac{1}{4}$ pint	142 ml	150 ml	1 oz	28.35 g	25 g
$\frac{1}{2}$ pint	284 ml	300 ml	2 oz	56.7 g	50 g
1 pint	568 ml	600 ml	4 oz	113.4 g	100 g
$1\frac{1}{2}$ pints	851 ml	900 ml	8 oz	226.8 g	225 g
$1\frac{3}{4}$ pints	992 ml	1 litre	12 oz	340.2 g	350 g
For quantities of $1\frac{3}{4}$ pints and over, litres and fractions of a litre have been used.			14 oz	397.0 g	400 g
			16 oz (1 lb)	453.6 g	450 g
			1 kilogram (kg) equals 2.2 lb.		

KEY TO SYMBOLS

⊙ Indicates a recipe which is quick to prepare and cook.

🥄 Indicates a recipe which is easy to prepare, but will take longer to cook.

⊙🥄 Indicates a recipe which is both quick and easy to make.

1.00* Indicates minimum preparation and cooking times in hours and minutes. They do not include prepared items in the list of ingredients; calcu-lated times apply only to the method. An asterisk * indicates extra time should be allowed, so check the note below symbols.

⌂ Chef's hats indicate degree of difficulty of a recipe: no hat means it is straightforward; one hat slightly more complicated; two hats indicates that it is for more advanced cooks.

£ Indicates a recipe which is good value for money; £ £ indicates an expensive recipe. No £ sign indicates an inexpensive recipe.

✳ Indicates that a recipe will freeze. If there is no symbol, the recipe is unsuitable for freezing. An asterisk * indicates special freezer instructions so check the note immediately below the symbols.

309 cals Indicates calories per serving, including any sugges-tions (e.g. cream, to serve) given in the ingredients.

QUICK AND EASY COOKING

Whether it's a demanding job that keeps you busy, children at home during the day, or a hectic social life, these days there's precious little time to spend in the kitchen, even for everyday meals, let alone for special occasions. The accent today is on fast food and convenience, but don't let this turn you away from home cooking altogether. This book is full of imaginative ideas to put the sparkle back in your cooking, without long lists of unusual ingredients and complicated cooking methods. All the recipes take about an hour to make, from simple everyday snacks, suppers, main courses and teatime treats to special dishes for when you're entertaining in a hurry. And as a special feature, there are five menus for informal occasions, which will give you entertaining ideas when there's no time for formal dinner parties.

At the back of the book you'll find pages and pages of information to help make life easier in the kitchen. Cooking techniques, information about the best equipment to buy to help you save time, how to get the best out of your freezer, plus handy hints and tricks of the trade to give your cooking a professional touch with clever presentation, garnishing and decoration. Then there's a handy reference section of basic recipes right at the end of the book—sauces and dressing, pastries, cakes and icing—which you can refer to at a glance when you're cooking in a hurry.

Everyday Main Meals

Time is always short during the week, and evening meals almost always prepared in a hurry. In this chapter you will find lots of ideas for last-minute main courses using quick-cooking cuts of meat such as mince, chops, offal and chicken portions — plus fish and eggs, which are the quickest cooking of all. And there are even a couple of puds, for when you have the time to give the family a midweek treat.

TAGLIATELLE BOLOGNESE ⊖ ✎

| 0.40 | ✳* | 725 cals |

* freeze Bolognese sauce after step 3

Serves 4

30 ml (2 tbsp) olive or other
    vegetable oil, plus 5 ml (1 tsp)

1 onion, skinned and chopped

1 garlic clove, skinned and
    crushed

2 rashers of streaky bacon, rinded
    and chopped

450 g (1 lb) minced beef

396 g (14 oz) can tomatoes

300 ml ($\frac{1}{2}$ pint) beef stock

30 ml (2 tbsp) red or white wine or
    wine vinegar

15 ml (1 tbsp) tomato purée

15 ml (1 tbsp) chopped fresh
    oregano or 5 ml (1 tsp) dried

15 ml (1 tbsp) chopped fresh mixed
    herbs or 5 ml (1 tsp) dried

1 bay leaf

pinch of sugar

salt and freshly ground pepper

400 g (14 oz) tagliatelle

freshly grated Parmesan cheese,
    to serve

1 Heat the 30 ml (2 tbsp) oil in a
heavy-based pan, add the
onion, garlic and bacon and fry
gently for 5 minutes until
softened.

2 Add the beef and fry for a
further 5 minutes until
browned, stirring constantly and
pressing with a wooden spoon to
break up any lumps.

3 Add the tomatoes, stock, wine
or vinegar and tomato purée
with the herbs, sugar and seasoning to taste. Bring to the boil,
stirring, then lower the heat and
simmer, half covered, for 20
minutes.

4 Meanwhile, cook the tagliatelle
in plenty of boiling salted
water, adding the 5 ml (1 tsp) of oil
to the water (this prevents the
pasta from sticking together). For
the timing, follow the packet instructions and cook until *al dente*
(tender, but firm to the bite).
Drain thoroughly and turn into a
warmed serving dish.

5 Taste and adjust the seasoning
of the Bolognese sauce, then
pour over the tagliatelle. Serve
immediately, with Parmesan
cheese handed separately.

Menu Suggestion

Tagliatelle Bolognese is so substantial that it needs nothing more
than a tossed green salad to
accompany or follow it.

**TAGLIATELLE
BOLOGNESE**

Tagliatelle are one of the most
common noodles eaten in Italy,
and they are widely available
outside Italy, both in fresh and
dried forms. Flat ribbon noodles,
they come in three main
varieties: plain; with egg
(*all'uovo*); and green (*verde*),
which are spinach-flavoured.
Sometimes you will see them
coiled into nests and called
tagliatelle a nidi—often with
the two colours of green and
white packed together. For this
recipe, you can use any kind of
tagliatelle, but remember that
the fresh pasta will have a much
shorter cooking time than the
dried variety.

TANGY CHOPS ⊖♪

| 0.45 | £ | 526 cals |

Serves 4

30 ml (2 tbsp) vegetable oil

4 lamb chump chops

salt and freshly ground pepper

finely grated rind and juice of 1
  lemon

30 ml (2 tbsp) chopped fresh
  parsley or 10 ml (2 tsp)
  dried parsley

15 ml (1 tbsp) chopped fresh mint
  or 5 ml (1 tsp) dried mint

5 ml (1 tsp) sugar

150 ml ($\frac{1}{4}$ pint) beef or chicken stock

1 Heat the oil in a sauté pan or
frying pan, add the chops and
fry over brisk heat until browned
on both sides. Lower the heat and
season the chops with salt and
pepper to taste.

2 Mix the remaining ingredients
together. Spoon this mixture
over the chops and pour in the
stock. Cover the pan tightly and
simmer gently for 30 minutes or
until the meat is tender. Serve hot
on a warmed dish, with the juices
poured over.

Menu Suggestion
Serve for an informal family meal
with grilled or oven-baked
tomatoes, potatoes and a seasonal
green vegetable.

ORIENTAL LAMB

| 1.00 | £ | 493 cals |

Serves 4

1.4 kg (3 lb) lean shoulder of lamb
450 g (1 lb) small new potatoes
225 g (8 oz) small pickling onions
30 ml (2 tbsp) vegetable oil
25 g (1 oz) butter or margarine
15 ml (1 tbsp) flour
5 ml (1 tsp) ground ginger
300 ml ($\frac{1}{2}$ pint) chicken stock
15 ml (1 tbsp) Worcestershire sauce
30 ml (2 tbsp) soy sauce
salt and freshly ground pepper
2 caps canned pimento, diced

1 Slice all the meat off the bone, discarding any excess fat, and cut into 2.5 cm (1 inch) pieces about 5 mm ($\frac{1}{4}$ inch) thick.

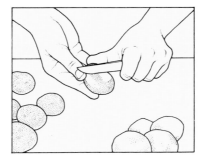

2 Wash the new potatoes and scrub them with a vegetable brush, or scrape with a knife.

3 Skin the onions. Put them in a bowl and pour in enough boiling water to cover. Leave to stand for 2 minutes, then drain and plunge into a bowl of cold water. Peel off the skin with your fingers.

4 Heat the oil and fat in a large sauté pan and brown the meat in it a few pieces at a time. Remove from the pan with a slotted spoon.

5 Add the potatoes and onions to the residual fat in the pan and fry them until lightly browned, turning frequently.

6 Return the meat to the pan, sprinkle in the flour and ginger and stir well. Cook gently, stirring, for 2 minutes.

7 Add the stock, Worcestershire sauce, soy sauce and seasoning to taste. Bring to the boil, stirring, then cover and simmer for 30 minutes or until the meat is tender.

8 Add the pimentos and stir over low heat to bring to serving temperature. Taste and adjust seasoning, then transfer to a warmed serving dish. Serve hot.

Menu Suggestion
This casserole has its own vegetables included with the meat. Serve with a simple green salad, or a seasonal green vegetable such as courgettes, if liked.

GLAZED GAMMON STEAKS ⊝ ✒

| 0.25 | £ | 753 cals |

Serves 4

15 ml (1 tbsp) soy sauce

2.5 ml (½ tsp) dry mustard

15 ml (1 tbsp) golden syrup

1.25 ml (¼ tsp) ground ginger

90 ml (6 tbsp) orange juice

garlic salt

freshly ground black pepper

15 ml (1 tbsp) cornflour

15 ml (1 tbsp) lemon juice

8 bacon chops or 4 gammon steaks

1 In a small saucepan, combine the first five ingredients, with garlic salt and pepper to taste.

2 Blend the cornflour with the lemon juice, stir in a little of the mixture from the pan and then return it all to the pan. Bring to the boil, stirring all the time, until the mixture has thickened to a glaze. Remove from the heat.

3 Cut most of the fat from the bacon chops or gammon steaks and then brush half of the glaze on one side.

4 Grill under moderate heat for 15 minutes, until the meat is cooked right through, brown and bubbling. Turn several times and brush with the remaining glaze during cooking. Serve hot.

Menu Suggestion

Serve with sauté potatoes and a medley of frozen vegetables such as peas, sweetcorn and peppers. Frozen stir-fried vegetables (available in packets from most supermarkets) make a good standby accompaniment when you are preparing a last-minute meal such as this one.

GLAZED GAMMON STEAKS

For everyday family meals and informal entertaining, bacon chops and gammon steaks are a good buy because they cook so quickly. They are also economical in that they have very little wastage in the form of fat or bone. For this recipe, a small amount of fat around the edges of the meat will help keep the meat moist during grilling. If you are using gammon steaks, it is a good idea to cut the fat at regular intervals to help prevent curling. Simply snip through the fat with sharp kitchen scissors, allowing about 5 mm (¼ inch) between cuts. This will give the finished dish an attractive professional touch, as well as helping the meat to cook more evenly.

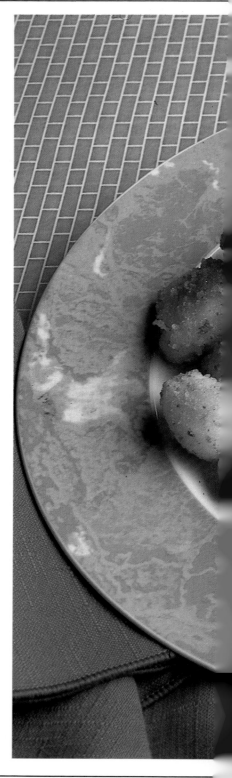

CRUMB TOPPED PORK CHOPS ⊙ ✎

1.00	£	408 cals

Serves 4

4 lean pork loin chops

50 g (2 oz) fresh white breadcrumbs

15 ml (1 tbsp) chopped fresh
   parsley or 5 ml (1 tsp)
   dried parsley

5 ml (1 tsp) chopped fresh mint or
   2.5 ml ($\frac{1}{2}$ tsp) dried mint

pinch of dried thyme

finely grated rind of 1 lemon

2.5 ml ($\frac{1}{2}$ tsp) coriander seeds,
   crushed

1 egg, beaten

salt and freshly ground pepper

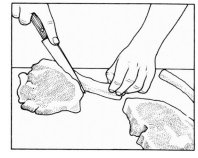

1 Cut the rind off the chops and
put them in one layer in a
baking tin.

2 Mix the remaining ingredients
together with seasoning to
taste. Spread this mixture evenly
over the chops with a palette knife.

3 Bake in the oven at 200°C
(400°F) mark 6 for about 45–
50 minutes, or until golden. Serve
hot, on a warmed dish.

Menu Suggestion
Serve with jacket-baked potatoes
(cooked in the oven at the same
time) and a vegetable dish which
has its own sauce such as
ratatouille or tomatoes in cream.

KIDNEY AND MUSHROOM SAUTÉ ⊖ ✎

| 0.15 | f | 208–277 cals |

Serves 3–4

450 g (1 lb) lamb's kidneys

15 ml (1 tbsp) vegetable oil

25 g (1 oz) butter

225 g (8 oz) large flat mushrooms, sliced

30 ml (2 tbsp) single cream

10 ml (2 tsp) whole grain mustard

1 garlic clove, skinned and crushed

salt and freshly ground pepper

chopped fresh parsley, to garnish

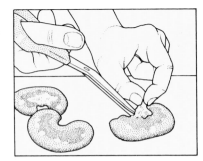

1 Skin each kidney, halve lengthways and snip out the core. Halve again.

2 Heat the oil and butter in a large frying pan until hot. Add the kidney pieces and fry quickly, turning them frequently, until browned on all sides.

3 Stir in the mushrooms and cook for 1 minute, shaking the pan from time to time. Lower the heat, add the cream, mustard, garlic and seasoning to taste and heat through gently. Serve immediately, garnished with parsley.

Menu Suggestion

Serve in a rice ring, with a mixed green side salad.

17

PAN-FRIED LIVER AND TOMATO ✎

| 0.15* | 290 cals |

* plus several hours marinating
Serves 4

450 g (1 lb) lamb's liver, sliced

30 ml (2 tbsp) Marsala or sweet sherry

salt and freshly ground pepper

225 g (8 oz) tomatoes, skinned

30 ml (2 tbsp) vegetable oil

2 medium onions, skinned and finely sliced

pinch of ground ginger

150 ml ($\frac{1}{4}$ pint) chicken stock

1 Using a very sharp knife, cut the liver into wafer-thin strips. Place in a shallow bowl with the Marsala or sweet sherry. Sprinkle with freshly ground pepper to taste. Cover and leave to marinate for several hours.

2 Cut the tomatoes into quarters and remove the seeds, reserving the juices. Slice the flesh into fine strips and set aside.

3 Heat the oil in a sauté pan or non-stick frying pan. When very hot, add the liver strips, a few at a time. Shake the pan briskly for about 30 seconds until pearls of blood appear.

4 Turn the slices and cook for a further 30 seconds only (liver hardens if it is overcooked). Remove from the pan with a slotted spoon and keep warm while cooking the remaining batches.

5 Add the onions and ginger to the residual oil in the pan and cook, uncovered, for about 5 minutes. Add the stock and seasoning to taste, return the liver to the pan and add the tomatoes and their juice. Bring just to the boil, then turn into a warmed serving dish and serve immediately.

Menu Suggestion
Serve with Chinese egg noodles and a stir-fried vegetable dish of onion, ginger, beansprouts and carrots.

PAN-FRIED LIVER AND TOMATO
The Marsala used in this recipe is an Italian fortified white wine, available at good off licences and some large supermarkets with good wine departments. The wine is named after the town of Marsala, in the western part of the island of Sicily in the Mediterranean, where it has been made for over two hundred years. It was first introduced into Britain by a Liverpool merchant, John Woodhouse, who set up a thriving business importing Marsala from Sicily—he even supplied Lord Nelson's fleet with it! There are different types of Marsala, from very dry to sweet. For this recipe, use one of the dry varieties.

GOLDEN BAKED CHICKEN ✎

| 1.15 | £ | 324 cals |

Serves 4

4 chicken portions

1 small onion, skinned and finely chopped

salt and freshly ground pepper

50 g (2 oz) fresh white breadcrumbs

15 ml (1 tbsp) chopped fresh parsley and thyme or 5 ml (1 tsp) dried mixed herbs

50 g (2 oz) butter or margarine, melted

1 Wipe the chicken portions and season well with salt and freshly ground pepper.

2 Mix the breadcrumbs with the onion and herbs.

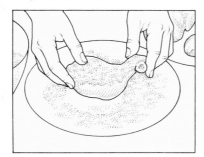

3 Brush the chicken joints all over with the butter or margarine; toss them in the herbed breadcrumbs and place in a buttered ovenproof dish.

4 Bake in the oven at 190°C (375°F) mark 5, for about 1 hour or until golden. Baste occasionally during cooking. Serve hot, straight from the dish.

Menu Suggestion
Serve with jacket-baked potatoes cooked in the oven at the same time, and a salad of tomato and raw onion with a lemony vinaigrette dressing.

FRENCH-STYLE ROAST CHICKEN

| 1.00 | £ | 349–465 cals |

Serves 3–4

1–1.4 kg (2¼–3 lb) oven ready
  chicken
5–6 sprigs fresh tarragon or parsley
  or 5 ml (1 tsp) dried tarragon or
  parsley
100 g (4 oz) butter, softened
salt and freshly ground pepper
150 ml (¼ pint) chicken stock
watercress, to garnish

1 Wipe the inside of the chicken, then put the tarragon or parsley inside it, with 15 g (½ oz) of the butter and some pepper.

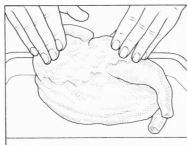

2 Place on one side in a roasting tin, smear all over with one third of the remaining butter and roast in the oven at 220°C (425°F) mark 7 for 15 minutes.

3 Turn the chicken onto the other side, smear with half the remaining butter and return to the oven. Roast for another 15 minutes.

4 Turn the chicken breast side up, smear with the rest of the butter, return to the oven and roast at 190°C (375°F) mark 5 for 20–30 minutes, or until tender.

5 Place the chicken on a serving dish and keep warm while making the gravy.

6 To make the gravy, place the roasting tin on top of the cooker and scrape any sediment sticking to the bottom. Add the stock and bring to the boil, then simmer for 2–3 minutes, stirring. Add seasoning to taste and pour into a warmed gravy boat. Garnish the chicken with watercress and serve immediately, with the gravy handed separately.

Menu Suggestion
Serve with the French potato dish *gratin dauphinois*—thinly sliced potatoes baked in a gratin dish with onion, cream and Gruyère cheese. Follow with a simple green salad tossed in vinaigrette dressing.

**FRENCH-STYLE
ROAST CHICKEN**

The French have a unique way of cooking chicken which gives a wonderfully moist and succulent flesh. The secret lies in smearing the bird with plenty of butter and turning it over at regular intervals during roasting. Tarragon has a natural affinity with chicken, and is the most popular herb to cook with it in France, so try to use it if you want an authentic 'French' flavour—it grows very easily in the garden in summer.

TURKEY AND BACON KEBABS

0.45* ✳* 551 cals

* plus at least 4 hours marinating;
freeze in the marinade

Serves 4

30 ml (2 tbsp) cranberry sauce

90 ml (6 tbsp) vegetable oil

45 ml (3 tbsp) freshly squeezed
orange juice

1 garlic clove, skinned and crushed

2.5 ml ($\frac{1}{2}$ tsp) ground allspice

salt and freshly ground pepper

700 g (1$\frac{1}{2}$ lb) boneless turkey
escalopes

1 small onion, skinned

1 large red pepper, cored, seeded
and cut into chunks

6 streaky bacon rashers, rinded and
halved

1 Put the cranberry sauce, oil
and orange juice in a shallow
dish with the garlic, allspice and
seasoning to taste. Whisk with a
fork until well combined.

2 Cut the turkey into bite-sized
pieces and place in the dish.
Stir to coat in the oil and orange
juice mixture, then cover and
leave to marinate for at least 4
hours. Stir the meat in the marinade occasionally during this time.

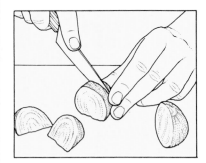

3 When ready to cook, cut the
onion into squares or even-
sized chunks.

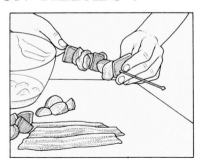

4 Thread the turkey, onion and
red pepper on to oiled skewers
with the bacon, dividing the ingredients as evenly as possible.

5 Grill under a preheated
moderate grill for about 20
minutes, turning the skewers frequently and basting with the remaining marinade. Serve hot.

Menu Suggestion

Make a quick, hot sauce to pour
over the kebabs by heating
together bottled cranberry sauce
with orange juice to taste. Serve
on a bed of saffron rice with a
chicory, orange and walnut salad
tossed in a sharp oil and vinegar
dressing.

**TURKEY AND BACON
KEBABS**

Turkey is lean and flavoursome,
but it has little natural fat, so it
can be dry if not prepared and
cooked in the correct way. The
marinade of oil and orange juice
in this recipe is an excellent way
of adding moisture to the flesh,
and the acid content of the
orange helps break down any
tough connective tissue. Don't
be tempted to omit the
marinating time if you are in a
hurry; the longer the turkey is
marinated the better. If it is
more convenient, the turkey can
be marinated in the refrigerator
overnight, but allow it to come to
room temperature before
grilling.

SEAFOOD STIR FRY ☺ ✓

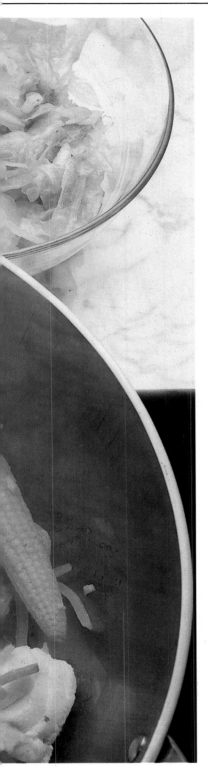

| 0.25 | £ | 288 cals |

Serves 4

2 celery sticks, washed and trimmed

1 medium carrot, peeled

350 g (12 oz) coley, haddock or cod fillet, skinned

350 g (12 oz) Iceberg or Cos lettuce

about 45 ml (3 tbsp) peanut oil

1 garlic clove, skinned and crushed

100 g (4 oz) peeled prawns

425 g (15 oz) can whole baby sweetcorn, drained

5 ml (1 tsp) anchovy essence

salt and freshly ground pepper

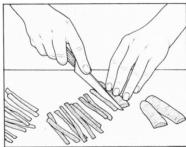

1 Slice the celery and carrot into thin matchsticks, 5 cm (2 inch) long. Cut the fish into 2.5 cm (1 inch) chunks.

2 Shred the lettuce finely with a sharp knife, discarding the core and any thick stalks.

3 Heat 15 ml (1 tbsp) of the oil in a wok or large frying pan until smoking. Add the lettuce and fry for about 30 seconds until lightly cooked. Transfer to a serving dish with a slotted spoon and keep warm in a low oven.

4 Heat another 30 ml (2 tbsp) of oil in the pan until smoking. Add the celery, carrot, white fish and garlic and stir-fry over high heat for 2–3 minutes, adding more oil if necessary.

5 Lower the heat, add the prawns, baby sweetcorn and anchovy essence. Toss well together for 2–3 minutes to heat through and coat all the ingredients in the sauce (the fish will flake apart).

6 Add seasoning to taste, spoon on top of the lettuce and serve immediately.

Menu Suggestion
This stir-fried dish has its own vegetables and therefore needs no further accompaniment other than a dish of plain boiled rice.

SEAFOOD STIR FRY

It may seem unusual to stir fry lettuce, which is usually only served as a raw salad vegetable, but it is a method often used in Chinese cookery. As long as you use the crisp varieties suggested here—Iceberg or Cos—you will find it gives a fresh, crunchy texture to the dish which contrasts well with the softness of the fish. Avoid using round or cabbage lettuces, which would become limp on cooking, and make sure to time the cooking accurately.

CREAMY COD BAKE ⊖ ✐

0.45	586 cals

Serves 4

454 g (1 lb) packet frozen leaf
  spinach

50 g (2 oz) butter or margarine

4 frozen cod steaks

2.5 ml (½ tsp) freshly grated nutmeg

salt and freshly ground pepper

450 ml (¾ pint) cheese sauce (see
  page 144)

100 g (4 oz) Cheddar cheese, grated

two 25 g (0.88 oz) packets cheese
  and onion crisps, finely crushed

1 Put the frozen spinach in a heavy-based saucepan and thaw over low heat, adding a few spoonfuls of water if necessary to prevent the spinach from sticking to the bottom of the pan.

2 Meanwhile, melt half the fat in a separate frying pan and fry the cod steaks for a few minutes on each side until golden.

3 Transfer the spinach to the base of an ovenproof dish and mix in the remaining fat with half the nutmeg and seasoning to taste.

4 Arrange the steaks in a single layer on top of the spinach and pour over any cooking juices.

5 Stir the remaining nutmeg into the cheese sauce, then pour the sauce evenly over the fish to cover it completely. Mix the grated cheese with the crushed crisps and sprinkle over the top.

6 Bake in the oven at 190°C (375°F) mark 5 for 30 minutes until golden brown and bubbling. Serve hot, straight from the dish.

Menu Suggestion
Serve with plain boiled or creamed potatoes. A few baked or grilled tomatoes as a vegetable accompaniment would add extra colour to the meal.

CREAMY COD BAKE

This is the perfect dish to serve for the children's lunch or supper—they will love the soft combination of spinach, fish and cheese sauce and its crunchy, crisp topping. Even if you normally find it difficult to persuade them to eat fish and spinach—with this dish they won't realise what they are eating!

Spinach is a nutritious vegetable. It is a valuable source of vitamins A and C, and has a high iron and calcium content. The frozen spinach used in this recipe is just as good as fresh and much quicker to prepare, but if you prefer to use the fresh vegetable, you will need double the quantity. Wash it thoroughly in several changes of water, discarding any yellow or damaged leaves and thick stalks. Place the leaves in a large saucepan with only the water that clings to them. Cook gently for about 7 minutes until tender, then drain very thoroughly and chop roughly. Continue with the recipe as for frozen spinach.

CURRIED EGGS ⊖ ✎

| 0.40 | £ | 214 cals |

Serves 4

30 ml (2 tbsp) vegetable oil

1 onion, skinned and chopped

1 medium cooking apple, peeled, cored and chopped

10 ml (2 tsp) garam masala

300 ml ($\frac{1}{2}$ pint) vegetable stock or water

225 g (8 oz) can tomatoes

15 ml (1 tbsp) tomato purée

2.5 ml ($\frac{1}{2}$ tsp) chilli powder

salt and freshly ground pepper

300 ml ($\frac{1}{2}$ pint) natural yogurt

4 eggs, hard-boiled

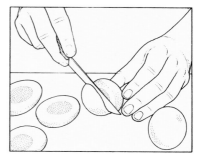

1 Heat the oil in a deep, heavy-based pan. Add the onion, apple and garam masala and fry gently until soft, stirring frequently.

2 Pour in the stock and tomatoes and bring to the boil, stirring to break up the tomatoes as much as possible. Stir in the tomato purée with the chilli powder and seasoning to taste. Lower the heat and simmer, uncovered, for 20 minutes to allow the flavours to develop.

3 Cool the sauce slightly, then pour into a blender or food processor. Add half of the yogurt and work to a purée. Return to the rinsed-out pan.

4 Shell the eggs and cut them in half lengthways. Add them to the sauce, cut side up, then simmer very gently for 10 minutes. Taste the sauce and adjust the seasoning if necessary. Serve hot, with the remaining yogurt drizzled over the top.

Menu Suggestion

Serve in a ring of boiled rice, accompanied by mango chutney and a cucumber salad dressed with natural yogurt and flavoured with fresh mint.

CURRIED EGGS

The Indian spice mixture, garam masala, is available in drums and jars from supermarkets and oriental specialist shops. You can use this ready-made mixture, but you will find your Indian dishes will taste fresher if you make your own garam masala. Ground spices quickly lose their essential oils, and you have no idea how long commercial brands of garam masala have been stored. If you make your own, make it in small quantities to suit your needs and store it in an airtight container. To make garam masala, crush 4 black or 10 green cardamoms, then put them in an electric mill or grinder with 15 ml (1 tablespoon) black peppercorns, 10 ml (2 teaspoons) cumin seeds, 2.5 cm (1 inch) cinnamon stick, 5 ml (1 tsp) cloves and 3 bay leaves. Grind to a fine powder.

BLACK FOREST TRIFLES ☺✎

0.20	266 cals

Serves 4

350 g (12 oz) fresh cherries or 425 g
  (15 oz) can cherries
½ packet (4) trifle sponges or 75 g
  (3 oz) sponge cake
150 ml (¼ pint) soured cream
15 ml (1 tbsp) kirsch or orange-
  flavoured liqueur (optional)
1 egg white
15 ml (1 tbsp) caster sugar
chocolate curls, to decorate

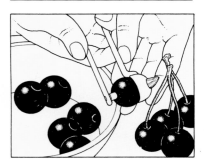

1 If using fresh cherries, stone
them, then simmer them
gently in a little water for 2–3
minutes. Leave to cool. If using
canned cherries, drain and stone
them, reserving the juice.

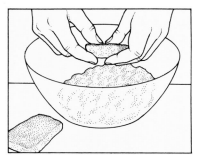

2 With your fingers, break the
trifle sponges or cake roughly
into a bowl. Stir in 30 ml (2 tbsp)
of the soured cream and the
liqueur, if using.

3 Divide the sponge mixture
between 4 stemmed glasses.
Spoon the cherries on top, with
120 ml (8 tbsp) of the cooking
liquid or reserved juices from the
canned cherries.

4 Whisk the egg white until stiff,
add the sugar and continue
whisking until very stiff. Fold into
the remaining soured cream.

5 Top each glass with the soured
cream mixture and chill in the
refrigerator until ready to serve.
Decorate with chocolate curls just
before serving.

Menu Suggestion
Exceptionally quick to prepare,
these trifles make a delicious
dessert for Sunday lunch, or even
Sunday tea when there's no time
to bake something special.

BLACK FOREST TRIFLES
Kirsch is a cherry brandy which
comes from the border area of
France, Germany and
Switzerland. The Germans call
their version *kirschwasser*, and
it is traditional to use it in the
famous Black Forest chocolate
and cherry gâteau,
Schwarzwalder Kirschtorte.
These Black Forest Trifles are a
variation on the theme, so the
addition of kirsch gives them
authenticity.

YOGURT AND ORANGE WHIP ☺✎

0.15	£	225 cals

Serves 4

2 eggs, separated
50 g (2 oz) caster sugar
finely grated rind of 1 orange
15 ml (1 tbsp) orange-flavoured
  liqueur
150 ml (¼ pint) natural yogurt
orange shreds, to decorate

1 In a deep bowl, whisk the egg
yolks with half of the sugar
until pale and creamy. Whisk in
the orange rind and liqueur.

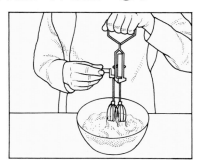

2 In a separate bowl, whisk the
egg whites until stiff but not
dry, add the rest of the sugar and
whisk again until stiff.

3 Fold the yogurt into the egg
yolk mixture, then fold in the
whisked egg whites until evenly
incorporated.

4 Spoon the mixture into 4
individual glasses and decorate
with orange shreds. Serve
immediately, or the mixture will
begin to separate.

Menu Suggestion
Yogurt and Orange Whip makes
the perfect last-minute cold
dessert. Serve with sponge fingers
or brandy snaps.

No Need to Cook

Making delicious meals without cooking must be the quickest and easiest method of all! Perfect for times when you're in a mad rush, or when the weather is hot and you don't relish the idea of cooking over a hot stove. This chapter is full of inspiring ideas for cold dishes, including smoked fish, a chilled summer soup and a choice of salads—and wonderful fresh fruity desserts.

SMOKED SALMON PÂTÉ ✓

| 0.30* | £ | 167 cals |

* plus 1½ hours chilling and 30 minutes standing

Serves 6

175 g (6 oz) smoked salmon 'off-cuts'

75 g (3 oz) unsalted butter, melted

20 ml (4 tsp) lemon juice

60 ml (4 tbsp) single cream

freshly ground pepper

cucumber slices, to garnish

150 ml (¼ pint) liquid aspic jelly

1 Roughly cut up the salmon pieces, reserving a few for garnishing, and place in a blender or food processor.

2 Add the butter, lemon juice and cream to the blender goblet or food processor.

3 Blend the mixture until it is smooth. Season to taste with freshly ground pepper. (Salt is not usually needed as smoked fish is salty enough.)

4 Spoon into a 300 ml (½ pint) dish to within 1 cm (½ inch) of the rim. Chill in the refrigerator for 1 hour to set.

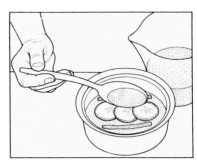

5 Garnish with the reserved pieces of smoked salmon and cucumber slices and spoon over the aspic jelly, which should be just on the point of setting. Refrigerate again for 30 minutes to set the aspic. Leave at room temperature for 30 minutes before serving.

Menu Suggestion
Serve for a dinner party starter with fingers of wholemeal or granary toast. Serve Duck with Mango (page 65) for the main course and Syllabub (page 66) for dessert.

SMOKED SALMON PÂTÉ

Real aspic jelly is made from stock, gelatine, wine, wine vinegar and egg whites. It is time-consuming to make because it has to be boiled time and time again until the liquid is clear, then filtered through a cloth or jelly bag before setting. Commercial aspic jelly powder, available in sachets at good supermarkets and delicatessens, makes a perfectly acceptable substitute for homemade aspic. Simply mix the powder with water until dissolved, then leave until on the point of setting before use. The amount of water required depends on the brand of powder used, so check the instructions on the sachet before using it. Aspic is useful for fish and meat pâtés alike.

SMOKED TROUT WITH TOMATOES AND MUSHROOMS. ☺ ✎

| 0.20* | 189 cals |

* plus 30 minutes to dégorge cucumber
Serves 8 as a starter

700 g (1½ lb) smoked trout
225 g (8 oz) cucumber, skinned
salt and freshly ground pepper
175 g (6 oz) mushrooms, wiped
45 ml (3 tbsp) creamed horseradish
30 ml (2 tbsp) lemon juice
60 ml (4 tbsp) natural yogurt
4 very large Marmande or
　　Beefsteak tomatoes, about 350 g
　　(12 oz) each
spring onion tops, to garnish

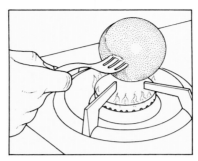

1 Flake the trout flesh, discarding the skin and bones.

2 Finely chop the cucumber, sprinkle with salt and leave for 30 minutes to dégorge. Rinse and drain well, then dry thoroughly with absorbent kitchen paper.

3 Finely chop the mushrooms, combine with the cucumber, horseradish, lemon juice and yogurt. Fold in the trout, then add seasoning to taste.

4 Skin the tomatoes. Pierce each one with a fork in the stalk end and then hold in the flame of a gas hob. Turn the tomato until the skin blisters and bursts, leave until cool enough to handle, then peel off the skin with your fingers.

5 Slice the tomatoes thickly, then sandwich in pairs with the trout mixture.

6 Arrange the tomato 'sandwiches' in a shallow serving dish. Garnish with snipped spring onion tops and chill in the refrigerator until ready to serve.

Menu Suggestion
Serve as a dinner party starter followed by Cheese Fondue (page 52) and a crisp green salad. Finish the meal with Mock Fruit Brûlées (page 69).

SMOKED TROUT WITH TOMATOES AND MUSHROOMS

For this recipe, it is important to buy the very large continental-type tomatoes. In the summer months these are widely available, some home-grown as well as the imported types from the Mediterranean. Look for them under the names 'Continental', 'Marmande' and 'Beefsteak' — any of these are suitable, as long as they are not too misshapen or they will not sandwich together. These types of tomatoes are also excellent stuffed.

MARINATED KIPPERS

0.20* | 395 cals

* plus at least 8 hours marinating
Serves 4

4 boneless kipper fillets
150 ml (¼ pint) olive oil
75 ml (5 tbsp) lemon juice
1.25 ml (¼ tsp) mustard powder
1 small onion, skinned and very finely chopped
1–2 garlic cloves, skinned and crushed
freshly ground pepper
a few raw onion rings, parsley sprigs and paprika, to garnish

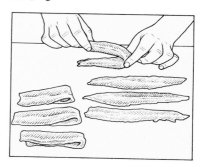

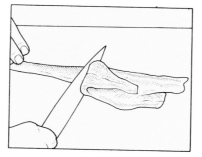

1 Skin the kipper fillets. Place them skin side down on a board, grip each one at the tail end and work the flesh away from the skin with a sharp knife, using a sawing motion.

2 In a jug, whisk together the remaining ingredients, except the garnish, adding pepper to taste.

3 Put the kippers in a shallow dish and pour over the marinade. Cover and chill in the refrigerator for at least 8 hours. Turn the kippers in the marinade occasionally during this time.

4 To serve, remove the kippers from the marinade and cut each one in half lengthways. Fold each half over crossways, then place in a single layer in a dish.

5 Pour the marinade over the kippers and garnish the top with onion rings, parsley sprigs and a sprinkling of paprika.

Menu Suggestion
Serve this chilled starter with granary bread or rolls and butter, and a bottle of dry white wine. Serve Beef with Stout (page 59) for the main course and Whisky Marinated Grapes (page 45) for dessert.

MARINATED KIPPERS
Kippers are herrings which are split and gutted, soaked in brine, then smoked. The best kippers are said to come from Loch Fyne in Scotland, although those from the Isle of Man are also considered to be very good. The choice of kippers is quite confusing—at fishmongers they are sold whole, boned, and as fillets, whereas in supermarkets they are available frozen as fillets and in vacuum 'boil-in-the-bag' packs. For this recipe you can use fresh or frozen fillets. Avoid buying those which are a deep, chestnut-brown colour as they have probably been dyed.

MEDITERRANEAN SUMMER SOUP ✓

| 0.45* | ✱* | 149 cals |

* plus at least 1 hour chilling; freeze
after step 4

Serves 4

2 very large Marmande or
    Beefsteak tomatoes

1 medium Spanish onion, skinned

1 green pepper, cored and seeded

450 g (1 lb) can potatoes, drained

4 garlic cloves, skinned

60 ml (4 tbsp) wine vinegar

1 litre (1¾ pints) water

30 ml (2 tbsp) olive oil

2.5 ml (½ tsp) paprika

salt and freshly ground pepper

a few ice cubes and fresh mint
    sprigs, to serve

1 Chop all the vegetables and
the garlic roughly and then put
half of them in a blender or food
processor with the vinegar and
about 150 ml (¼ pint) of the
measured water. Work to a
smooth purée.

2 Sieve the purée to remove the
tomato skins, working it into a
large soup tureen or bowl.

3 Repeat the puréeing and
sieving with the remaining
vegetables and another 150 ml
(¼ pint) of the water. Add to the
purée in the tureen or bowl.

4 Pour the remaining water into
the soup and add the oil,
paprika and seasoning to taste.
Stir well to mix, cover and chill in
the refrigerator for at least 1 hour
before serving.

5 To serve, taste and adjust the
seasoning, then stir in the ice
cubes. Float mint sprigs on top.

Menu Suggestion
Serve as a starter for a summer
luncheon or barbecue party, with
bowls of garnish such as tiny
bread croûtons (fried or toasted),
diced red and green pepper, diced
cucumber and finely chopped
hard-boiled eggs.

MEDITERRANEAN SUMMER SOUP

To make croûtons for floating on
top of this soup: remove the
crusts from 3 slices of stale white
bread. Cut the bread into dice,
then deep-fry in hot oil until
golden brown and crisp. Remove
with a slotted spoon and drain on
absorbent kitchen paper. For
toasted croûtons, toast the crust-
less bread first, then cut into
dice. Croûtons can be successfully frozen.

    For a professional touch, try
cutting the bread or toast into
different shapes with tiny aspic
jelly cutters, available from
specialist kitchen shops and
catering suppliers.

TURKEY ROQUEFORT SALAD ☺ 🥄

| 0.15* | 375 cals |

* plus 30 minutes chilling

Serves 4

150 ml ($\frac{1}{4}$ pint) soured cream

100 g (4 oz) Roquefort or any other
　blue cheese, crumbled

salt and freshly ground pepper

450 g (1 lb) cold cooked turkey,
　skinned and cut into pieces

lettuce or endive leaves, washed
　and trimmed

snipped chives, to garnish

1 Mix the soured cream and
Roquefort together to make a
dressing. Season to taste. Add the
turkey and coat well in it. Cover
and chill in the refrigerator for 30
minutes.

2 To serve, arrange the lettuce
or endive leaves in a serving
bowl. Spoon the turkey mixture in
the centre and sprinkle with
chives. Serve chilled.

Menu Suggestion
Serve for a summer luncheon with
fresh French bread or rolls and a
bottle of dry sparkling white wine.

HAM AND CHEESE SALAD WITH AVOCADO ⊖ ✓

0.15	£ £	502 cals

Serves 4

2 ripe avocados

60 ml (4 tbsp) natural yogurt

1 garlic clove, skinned and crushed

a few drops of Tabasco sauce

salt and freshly ground pepper

225 g (8 oz) lean cooked ham, cubed

225 g (8 oz) Emmenthal or Gruyère cheese, cubed

1 red pepper, cored, seeded and diced

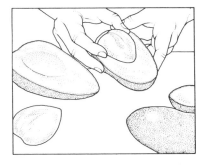

1 Halve the avocados and remove the stones, then peel and mash the flesh. Mix quickly with the yogurt, garlic and Tabasco, seasoning to taste.

2 Fold the ham, cheese and red pepper (reserving some pepper to garnish) into this dressing and pile into a salad bowl. Serve immediately, or the avocado flesh may discolour the dressing. Sprinkle with the reserved red pepper.

Menu Suggestion
This salad is incredibly quick to prepare. Serve it for a healthy lunch, with granary bread rolls.

WHISKY MARINATED GRAPES

| 0.30* | f | 99–230 cals |

* plus at least 4 hours marinating
and 30 minutes chilling

Serves 6

350 g (12 oz) black grapes
350 g (12 oz) green grapes
30 ml (2 tbsp) whisky
45 ml (3 tbsp) clear honey
5 ml (1 tsp) lemon juice

1 Wash the grapes, drain well
and dry with absorbent
kitchen paper.

2 Cut the grapes carefully in half
lengthways, then ease out the
pips with the point of a knife.

3 In a large mixing bowl, stir
together the whisky, honey
and lemon juice. Add the grapes
and stir well. Cover with cling film
and leave in a cool place (not the
refrigerator) to marinate for at
least 4 hours, preferably
overnight.

4 Spoon into a serving dish and
chill in the refrigerator for 30
minutes before serving. Serve with
Yogurt Cream.

YOGURT CREAM

150 ml (¼ pint) extra thick double
　　cream
150 ml (¼ pint) natural yogurt
pinch of sugar (optional)

1 Lightly whip the cream, then
fold together with the yogurt
and sugar.

2 Spoon into a serving dish,
cover and chill well.

Menu Suggestion
Light, luscious and fruity, this
dessert is perfect after a heavy or
rich main course such as Beef with
Stout (page 59) or Boeuf
Stroganoff (page 56).

WHISKY MARINATED GRAPES

Grapes, the fruits of the vine,
come in two different colours,
green (white) and black, but
there are numerous different
varieties cultivated in warm,
sunny climates all over the
world. Besides the dessert grapes
used here, there are also wine
grapes, and grapes cultivated
specifically for drying—to make
raisins, currants and sultanas.
Dessert grapes for eating are the
sweetest of all the varieties;
green ones vary from bright
green to yellow, whereas black
grapes can be pink, purple, red
or blue-black. When choosing
grapes for eating, avoid fruit
which is shiny; fresh grapes
should have a powdery whitish
bloom on their skin. For this
recipe, try to buy the seedless
green grapes, which will save you
time on preparation. Good black
varieties to look for are Gamay,
Black Hamburg and Waltham
Cross. It is a good idea to try
grapes before buying them.

STRAWBERRIES WITH RASPBERRY SAUCE

0.20*	91 cals

* plus at least 30 minutes chilling

Serves 6

900 g (2 lb) small strawberries

450 g (1 lb) raspberries

50 g (2 oz) icing sugar

1 Hull the strawberries and place them in individual serving dishes.

2 Purée the raspberries in a blender or food processor until just smooth, then work through a nylon sieve into a bowl to remove the pips.

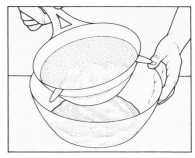

3 Sift the icing sugar over the bowl of raspberry purée, then whisk in until evenly incorporated. Pour over the strawberries. Chill in the refrigerator for at least 30 minutes before serving.

Menu Suggestion

This dessert is so simple to make, yet it's absolutely delicious. Serve it at a summer dinner party after an equally simple main course such as Italian Marinated Trout (page 55).

STRAWBERRIES WITH RASPBERRY SAUCE

Freshly picked raspberries freeze successfully (unlike strawberries which tend to lose texture and shape due to their high water content). If you have raspberries which are slightly overripe or misshapen, the best way to freeze them is as a purée; this takes up less space in the freezer and is immensely useful for making quick desserts and sauces at the last minute. For this recipe, for example, you can freeze the purée up to 12 months in advance, then it will only take a few minutes to put the dessert together after the purée has thawed. The purée can be frozen with or without the icing sugar.

ORANGE SHERBET

| 0.10* | £ | 268 cals |

* plus 4–5 hours freezing

Serves 8

178 ml (6¼ oz) carton frozen orange
 juice

175 g (6 oz) caster sugar

45 ml (3 tbsp) golden syrup

45 ml (3 tbsp) lemon juice

568 ml (1 pint) milk

300 ml (½ pint) single cream

shreds of orange rind and sprigs of
 mint, to decorate

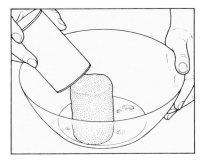 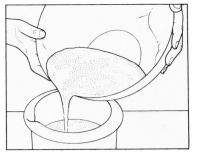

1 Tip the frozen, undiluted
orange juice into a deep bowl.
Leave until beginning to soften,
then add the sugar, golden syrup
and lemon juice. Whisk until
smooth.

2 Combine the orange mixture
with the milk and cream and
pour into a deep, rigid container.
Cover and freeze for 4–5 hours.
There is no need to whisk the
mixture during freezing.

3 Transfer to the refrigerator to
soften 45 minutes–1 hour
before serving. Serve scooped into
individual glasses or orange shells,
decorated with orange shreds and
sprigs of mint.

Menu Suggestion
Make up a batch or two and keep
in the freezer for dinner parties. It
makes a tangy and refreshing end
to a rich meal.

ORANGE SHERBET
There is always some confusion
over the term 'sherbet' when
used to describe a dessert. The
word 'sherbet' is in fact the
American term for a sorbet,
although it is often mistakenly
used to describe a water ice.
Water ices are simple con-
coctions of sugar syrup and fruit
purée or fruit juice, sometimes
with liqueur or other alcohol
added. Sorbets are a smoother
version of water ices. They are
made in the same way, with
sugar syrup and fruit, but at the
half-frozen stage they have
whisked egg whites or other
ingredients folded into them.

Mid-week Entertaining

If you've invited guests to eat during the week, it's unlikely you will have much time to prepare and cook beforehand. A certain amount of preparation can be done in advance, but what you really need are dishes that are both quick and easy to prepare, and yet with such delicious results that everyone will think you've spent hours in the kitchen. Here you will find lots of lightning-quick dishes that will fool even the most discerning of guests!

AVOCADO WITH CRAB

0.25	£ £	576 cals

Serves 4

30 ml (2 tbsp) vegetable oil

1 small onion, skinned and very
    finely chopped

10 ml (2 tsp) garam masala

150 ml ($\frac{1}{4}$ pint) thick homemade
    mayonnaise (see page 151)

10 ml (2 tsp) tomato purée

finely grated rind and juice of $\frac{1}{2}$
    a lemon

salt and freshly ground pepper

225 g (8 oz) white crab meat

2 ripe avocados

lemon twists and paprika,
    to garnish

1 Make the filling. Heat the oil
in a small pan, add the onion
and garam masala and fry gently,
stirring constantly, for 5 minutes
until the onion is soft. Turn into a
bowl and leave until cold.

2 Add the mayonnaise to the
cold onion with the tomato
purée, lemon rind and juice. Add
seasoning to taste.

3 Flake the crab meat and fold
gently into the mayonnaise,
taking care not to break up the
pieces of crab.

4 Cut the avocados in half
lengthways and then prise the
halves apart by twisting them in
opposite directions.

5 Remove the stones from the
avocados by gently easing
them out with the fingers.

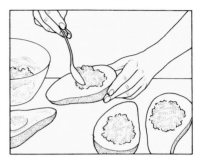

6 Place an avocado half on each
serving dish or plate, then pile
the filling into each half. Garnish
with lemon twists, a sprinkling of
paprika, and serve immediately.

Menu Suggestion
Serve for a dinner party starter
with brown bread and butter and
chilled dry white wine. Follow
with Cheese Fondue (page 52) and
Strawberries with Raspberry
Sauce (page 46).

AVOCADO WITH CRAB
Crab is expensive, whether fresh,
frozen or canned. For this
recipe you can use any kind, but
you will probably find the most
economical way to buy it is as
dressed crab (in its shell). To
make the white meat go further,
you can of course use some of
the dark meat, but take care not
to use too much as the flavour
of dark meat is rather strong.
Dark crab meat is best reserved
for sandwiches when it can be
combined with other ingredients
which will temper its richness.

MELON WITH PORT 🥄

| 0.15* | £ £ | 124 cals |

* plus at least 1 hour chilling

Serves 4

2 small Charentais, Cantaloupe or Ogen melons

180 ml (12 tbsp) port wine

sprigs of mint, to garnish

1 Halve the melons horizontally, trimming the bases so they will stand firmly. Scoop out the seeds with a teaspoon and discard.

2 Pour 45 ml (3 tbsp) of port wine into each half. Cover tightly with cling film and chill in the refrigerator for at least 1 hour.

3 Serve garnished with sprigs of fresh mint.

Menu Suggestion
Serve as a starter for a special dinner party followed by a main course of Cheese and Anchovy Grilled Chicken Breasts (page 64) and Syllabub (page 66).

CELERIAC RÉMOULADE ⊙ 🥄

0.15	480 cals

Serves 6

1 large head celeriac
30 ml (2 tbsp) lemon juice
300 ml (½ pint) homemade
   mayonnaise (see page 145)
30 ml (2 tbsp) snipped chives
30 ml (2 tbsp) French mustard
salt and freshly ground pepper
1 lettuce or curly endive
chopped fresh parsley, to garnish

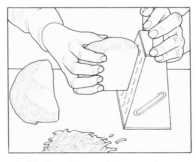

1 Peel and coarsely grate the celeriac. Toss immediately in the lemon juice to prevent discoloration.

2 Add the mayonnaise, chives and mustard with seasoning to taste and mix well together.

3 Line individual dishes or plates with lettuce, then pile the celeriac mixture in the centre. Sprinkle with chopped parsley and serve immediately.

Menu Suggestion
Serve as a starter with hot garlic bread. Follow with a main course of Pork Escalopes with Juniper (page 63) and Mock Fruit Brûlées (page 69) for dessert.

CHEESE FONDUE ⊖ ✎

| 0.20 | £ £ | 874 cals |

Serves 6

450 g (1 lb) Gruyère cheese
450 g (1 lb) Emmenthal cheese
30 ml (2 tbsp) cornflour
1 garlic clove, skinned
450 ml (¾ pint) dry white wine
1 liqueur glass of kirsch (optional)
freshly ground pepper
pinch of grated nutmeg
1 loaf French bread, cubed

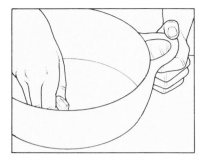

1 Grate the Gruyère and Emmenthal cheeses and mix together with the cornflour.

2 Rub the inside of a heavy-based flameproof dish with the garlic. Put the cheese in the dish and add the wine.

3 Heat gently, stirring all the time until the cheese has melted. Add the kirsch, if using, and season with freshly ground pepper and nutmeg. Stir well together. When the mixture is of a thick creamy consistency, it is ready to serve.

4 Pile the bread cubes into a basket and serve with the fondue.

Menu Suggestion
Serve this unusual Swiss dish as a main course for an informal supper party. Strawberries with Raspberry Sauce (page 46) would make a perfect finale to the meal.

CHEESE FONDUE
Fondue is usually prepared in a glazed earthenware dish with a handle. Traditionally it is served at the table in the dish in which it was cooked and kept warm over a small spirit lamp or dish-warmer. To eat it, the cubes of crusty bread are speared on long forks and dipped in the fondue. If you like, small glasses of kirsch can be served with the fondue—guests should dip the cubes of bread first in the kirsch, before dipping in the fondue.

ITALIAN MARINATED TROUT

0.15* £ £ 221 cals

* plus at least 8 hours marinating

Serves 4

30 ml (2 tbsp) olive oil

4 whole trout, about 225 g (8 oz) each, cleaned

30 ml (2 tbsp) flour

1 small bulb Florence fennel, trimmed and finely sliced

1 onion, skinned and finely sliced

300 ml (½ pint) dry white Italian wine

finely grated rind and juice of 1 orange

salt and freshly ground pepper

orange slices and chopped fennel tops, to garnish

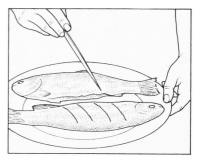

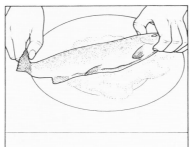

1 Heat the olive oil in a frying pan. Dip the trout in the flour and fry gently for 4 minutes on each side. With a fish slice, transfer the fish to a shallow dish.

2 With a sharp knife, score the skin diagonally, being careful not to cut too deeply into the flesh. Set aside.

3 Add the fennel and onion to the frying pan and fry for 5 minutes. Add the wine, orange rind and juice, and seasoning to taste. Bring to the boil. Boil rapidly for 1 minute, add the chopped fennel tops and pour immediately over the fish. Cool.

4 Marinate in the refrigerator for at least 8 hours, but no more than 3 days.

5 Serve at room temperature, garnished with orange slices and the chopped fennel tops.

Menu Suggestion

Serve for a cold summer supper party with hot garlic or herb bread and a mixed salad. Follow with Strawberries with Raspberry Sauce (page 46) for dessert.

ITALIAN MARINATED TROUT

The bulb vegetable Florence fennel looks rather like a squat version of celery with feathery leaves. The flavour of fennel is like aniseed; for the most subtle taste of aniseed, buy white or pale green fennel, for a stronger flavour, choose vegetables which are dark green in colour. In this recipe, fennel is fried with onion and used in a marinade for fish, with which it has a particular affinity. Other more usual uses for fennel are sliced or chopped raw in salads (fennel and tomato are particularly good together), and braised in the oven with stock or a white or cheese sauce. As its name suggests, Florence fennel comes from Italy, where it is used extensively in cooking.

BOEUF STROGANOFF
(BEEF WITH MUSHROOMS AND SOURED CREAM)

| 0.25 | £ £ | 538 cals |

Serves 4

700 g (1½ lb) rump steak, thinly
    sliced

45 ml (3 tbsp) flour

salt and freshly ground pepper

50 g (2 oz) butter

1 onion, skinned and thinly sliced

225 g (8 oz) mushrooms, wiped and
    sliced

150 ml (¼ pint) soured cream

10 ml (2 tsp) tomato purée
    (optional)

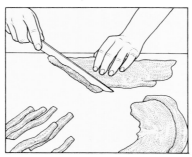

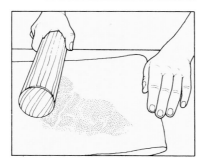

1 Beat the steak with a meat
mallet or rolling pin between
two sheets of greaseproof paper.

2 Trim the fat off the steak and
discard. Cut the meat across
the grain into thin strips.

3 Coat the strips of steak in the
flour seasoned with salt and
pepper. Melt half the butter in a
sauté pan, add the meat and fry
for 5–7 minutes, tossing
constantly until golden brown.

4 Add the remaining butter, the
onion and mushrooms and fry,
stirring, for 3–4 minutes. Stir in
the soured cream and tomato
purée (if liked), and season well,
using plenty of pepper. Heat
through gently, without boiling.
Transfer to a warmed serving dish
and serve immediately.

Menu Suggestion
Boeuf Stroganoff is a rich main
course dish for a dinner party.
Serve Celeriac Rémoulade (page
51) to start, and end with Whisky
Marinated Grapes (page 45).

BOEUF STROGANOFF

The story goes that this dish was
created in the nineteenth century
by a French chef for a Russian
nobleman called Count
Stroganoff. The chef worked for
the Count, who was something
of a gourmet. In the freezing
temperatures of the Russian
winter, there were always
problems cutting meat, which
was more or less permanently
frozen. On one occasion when
the Count ordered beef, the chef
hit upon the idea of cutting it
into wafer-thin slices—this way
it was easier to cut and it also
cooked more quickly. The result
of this experiment has since
become a famous, classic dish, so
it must have met with the
Count's approval!

BEEF WITH STOUT

| 2.30 | £ ✳ | 509 cals |

Serves 4

700 g (1½ lb) stewing beef

30 ml (2 tbsp) vegetable oil

2 large onions, skinned and sliced

15 ml (1 tbsp) flour

275 ml (9.68 fl oz) can stout

200 ml (7 fl oz) beef stock

30 ml (2 tbsp) tomato purée

100 g (4 oz) stoned prunes

225 g (8 oz) carrots, peeled and sliced

salt and freshly ground pepper

croûtons, to garnish

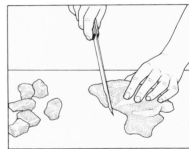

1 Cut the meat into 4 cm (1½ inch) cubes, trimming off all fat. Heat the oil in a flameproof casserole, add the meat and fry until well browned on all sides. Remove with a slotted spoon.

2 Add the onions to the remaining oil in the pan and fry gently until lightly browned. Stir in the flour and cook for 1 minute. Stir in the stout, stock, tomato purée, prunes and carrots. Bring to the boil and season well.

3 Replace the meat, cover and cook in the oven at 170°C (325°F) mark 3 for 1½–2 hours until tender. Adjust seasoning. Serve garnished with croûtons.

Menu Suggestion
Start with Celeriac Rémoulade (page 51) and end with Whisky Marinated Grapes (page 45).

LAMB NOISETTES WITH RED WINE SAUCE ✓

| 1.00 | £ £ | 617 cals |

Serves 6

12 lamb noisettes

flour, for coating

25 g (1 oz) butter

60 ml (4 tbsp) vegetable oil

2 large onions, skinned and sliced

1 garlic clove, skinned and finely chopped

225 g (8 oz) button mushrooms, wiped

300 ml ($\frac{1}{2}$ pint) red wine

150 ml ($\frac{1}{4}$ pint) chicken stock

15 ml (1 tbsp) tomato purée

2 bay leaves

salt and freshly ground pepper

1 Lightly coat the lamb noisettes with flour. Heat the butter and oil in a large flameproof casserole. Add the noisettes, a few at a time, and brown quickly on both sides. Remove from the casserole with a slotted spoon and set aside.

2 Add the onion and garlic to the casserole and fry for about 5 minutes until golden. Add the mushrooms and fry for a further 2–3 minutes. Stir in the red wine, stock, tomato purée and bay leaves. Season well with salt and freshly ground pepper.

3 Replace the noisettes and bring to the boil, then cover and simmer gently for about 40 minutes until tender, turning the meat once during this time.

4 Lift the noisettes out of the sauce and remove the string. Place the noisettes on a warmed serving dish and keep warm. Boil the remaining liquid rapidly for 5–10 minutes to reduce the sauce. Taste and adjust the seasoning, then pour over the noisettes. Serve immediately.

Menu Suggestion
For a supper party, serve with Celeriac Rémoulade (page 51) to start, and Gooseberry Macaroon Crunch (page 70) for the dessert.

LAMB NOISETTES WITH RED WINE SAUCE

Lamb noisettes are a very special cut of meat. You can buy them ready-prepared at some large supermarkets, or ask your butcher to prepare them for you as they are a little tricky to do yourself. Lamb noisettes are cut from the best end of neck. This is the same cut which is used for making Guard of Honour, except that the bones are removed from the whole rack, then the meat is rolled up and tied at intervals according to how many cutlets there were in the rack—usually six or eight.

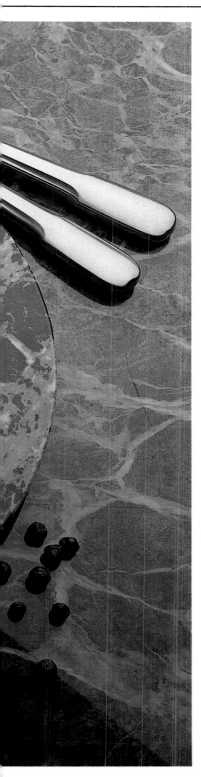

PORK ESCALOPES WITH JUNIPER ⊖ ✦

| 0.20 | £ £ | 646 cals |

Serves 4

450 g (1 lb) pork fillet (tenderloin)
40 g (1¼ oz) seasoned flour
25 g (1 oz) butter
75 ml (5 tbsp) dry white wine
4 juniper berries, lightly crushed
150 ml (¼ pint) double cream
salt and freshly ground pepper
chopped fresh parsley, to garnish

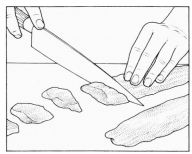

1 Trim any fat from the pork fillet and cut the meat into 5 mm (¼ inch) slices. Bat out into even thinner slices between two sheets of dampened greaseproof paper, using a meat cleaver or a wooden rolling pin.

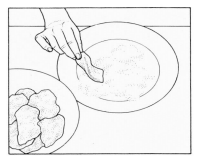

2 Dip the pork escalopes in the seasoned flour and shake off any excess.

3 Heat the butter in a large frying pan and fry the escalopes briskly for 2 minutes on each side. Remove and keep warm in a low oven while making the wine and cream sauce.

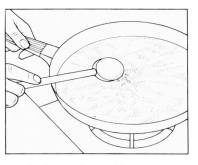

4 Add the wine and juniper berries to the pan and boil rapidly, scraping the bottom of the pan to loosen any sediment, until reduced by half. Pour in the cream, season to taste and bring to the boil. Boil rapidly for 1 minute, stirring. Pour over the escalopes and serve immediately, garnished with chopped parsley.

Menu Suggestion
The juniper berries cut the richness of the creamy sauce. Serve with French beans and steamed potatoes. Start with Melon with Port (page 50) and finish with Gooseberry Macaroon Crunch (page 70).

PORK ESCALOPES WITH JUNIPER

Juniper berries are round, purple-brown berries which look similar to peppercorns except that they are slightly larger and have smooth skin. They are not always easy to obtain in jars in supermarkets, so look for them in a health food shop or continental delicatessen. In the Mediterranean, they are a favourite spice to flavour pork and game dishes, and are often used in pâtés and terrines made with these meats.

CHEESE AND ANCHOVY GRILLED CHICKEN BREASTS ✎

1.00	£ £	511 cals

Serves 6

50 g (2 oz) can anchovy fillets in oil

30 ml (2 tbsp) finely chopped onion

5 ml (1 tsp) lemon juice

6 chicken breasts

vegetable oil, for brushing

225 g (8 oz) Mozzarella cheese, sliced

1 Drain 15 ml (1 tbsp) of the oil from the anchovy can into a small saucepan. Chop the anchovies finely.

2 Heat the anchovy oil, add the anchovies and onion and cook for about 5 minutes, until a paste forms. Stir in the lemon juice, then remove from the heat and leave to cool.

3 Lift the skin from each chicken breast and rub 5 ml (1 tsp) of the anchovy mixture on the flesh underneath the skin.

4 Put the chicken pieces, skin side down, on to a rack placed over the grill pan. Grill under moderate heat for 35–45 minutes until tender, turning once. Brush with oil occasionally during cooking, to moisten.

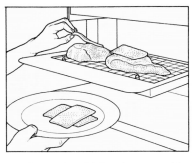

5 Cover the chicken breasts with slices of cheese and grill for a further 5 minutes, or until the cheese begins to bubble.

Menu Suggestion

For a midweek dinner party with these chicken breasts as the main course, serve Melon with Port (page 50) to start, and Syllabub (page 66) to finish.

CHEESE AND ANCHOVY GRILLED CHICKEN BREASTS

Anchovies tend to be rather salty. If you have the time when preparing this dish, it helps to soak the anchovies first, to remove excess salt. Simply drain the oil from the can, then place the anchovy fillets in a shallow dish. Pour over just enough milk to cover, then leave to soak for 20–30 minutes. Drain thoroughly and pat dry. The anchovies are now ready for use.

DUCK WITH MANGO ☉ ✐

| 0.35 | £ £ | 683 cals |

Serves 4

1 ripe, but still firm mango

4 duck portions, about 275 g (10 oz) each

60 ml (4 tbsp) peanut oil

2.5 ml (½ tsp) ground allspice

45 ml (3 tbsp) plum jam

20 ml (4 tsp) wine vinegar

salt and freshly ground pepper

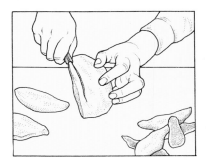

1 Skin and thickly slice the mango on either side of the large central stone.

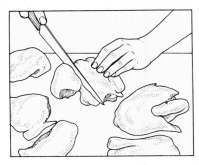

2 Remove any excess fat from the duck portions. Divide each portion into three and place in a saucepan. Cover with cold water and bring to the boil. Lower the heat and simmer gently for 15–20 minutes. Drain well and pat dry with absorbent kitchen paper. Trim bones.

3 Heat the oil in a wok or large frying pan until hot and smoking. Add the duck pieces and allspice. Brown well on all sides.

4 Stir in the plum jam and wine vinegar. Cook for a further 2–3 minutes, stirring constantly, until well glazed. Stir in the mango slices with seasoning to taste. Heat through, then turn into a warmed serving dish and serve immediately.

Menu Suggestion
Duck with Mango is a very special dinner party dish. Serve Avocado with Crab (page 49) to start, and Syllabub (page 66) to finish.

SYLLABUB

$\boxed{0.15*}$ $\boxed{300 \text{ cals}}$

* plus 3 hours infusing and 2 hours chilling

Serves 6

150 ml ($\frac{1}{4}$ pint) dry white wine

10 ml (2 tsp) finely grated lemon rind

30 ml (2 tbsp) lemon juice

75 g (3 oz) caster sugar

300 ml ($\frac{1}{2}$ pint) double cream

1 Pour the wine into a bowl. Add the lemon rind and juice and the sugar and stir well to mix. Leave at cool room temperature to infuse for at least 3 hours.

2 Add the cream and whip until the mixture is softly stiff and holds its shape. Do not overwhip or the mixture may curdle.

3 Pile into 6 individual glasses or glass dishes. Chill the syllabub in the refrigerator for 2 hours before serving.

Menu Suggestion
Syllabub is rich and creamy, with a tangy bite to it. Serve after a substantial, meaty main course such as Beef with Stout (page 59).

MOCK FRUIT BRÛLÉES ✎

| 0.35* | £ £ | 314 cals |

* plus overnight chilling and 1 hour chilling before serving

Serves 6

6 large, ripe peaches
30 ml (2 tbsp) lemon juice
150 ml ($\frac{1}{4}$ pint) double cream
30 ml (2 tbsp) icing sugar
30 ml (2 tbsp) almond-flavoured liqueur or a few drops of almond essence
150 ml ($\frac{1}{4}$ pint) soured cream
90–120 ml (6–8 tbsp) demerara sugar

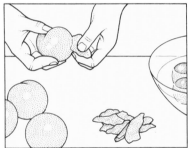

1 Skin the peaches. Dip them in a bowl of boiling water for 30 seconds, then drain and plunge immediately into a bowl of cold water. Carefully peel off the skins.

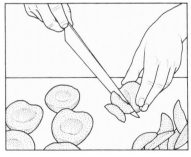

2 Cut the peaches in half. Twist them to separate and remove the stones. Thinly slice the flesh. Toss in lemon juice.

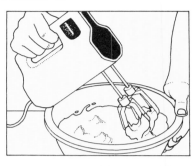

3 Whip the double cream with the icing sugar until it just holds its shape. Gradually whisk in the liqueur or almond essence. Fold in the soured cream and peach slices.

4 Divide the mixture equally between six 150 ml ($\frac{1}{4}$ pint) ramekin dishes. Cover and chill in the refrigerator overnight.

5 Sprinkle the demerara sugar evenly on top of each ramekin, to completely cover the peaches and cream mixture. Place under a preheated hot grill for 3–4 minutes until the sugar becomes caramelised. Chill thoroughly in the refrigerator for at least 1 hour before serving.

Menu Suggestion
Deceptively rich, these Mock Fruit Brûlées are best served after a light main course such as Italian Marinated Trout (page 55).

GOOSEBERRY MACAROON CRUNCH

0.25* | 321 cals

* plus several hours chilling

Serves 6

450 g (1 lb) gooseberries, topped
  and tailed

30 ml (2 tbsp) water

100 g (4 oz) caster sugar

30 ml (2 tbsp) kirsch

100 g (4 oz) French almond
  macaroons (ratafias), crumbled

150 ml (¼ pint) whipping cream

3 macaroons or 6 ratafias,
  to decorate

1 Cook the gooseberries with the water and sugar for 10–15 minutes until the fruit is soft and well reduced, then sieve it. Stir in the kirsch. Chill for 30 minutes.

2 Arrange the macaroon crumbs and gooseberry purée in alternate layers in 6 tall glasses. Chill in the refrigerator for several hours for the flavours to mellow.

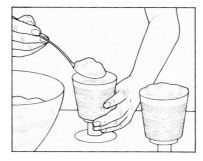

3 Whip the cream until it barely holds its shape. Spoon some of the soft cream over each glass and top each with a halved macaroon or whole ratafias. Serve immediately.

Menu Suggestion

Serve this pretty layered dessert for a mid-week dinner party after a starter of Melon with Port (page 50), and a main dish of Pork Escalopes with Juniper (page 63).

GOOSEBERRY MACAROON CRUNCH

There are many variations of this pretty dessert. According to seasonal availability, you can use different fruit from the gooseberries and an alternative liqueur to the kirsch. For example, cherries and kirsch would go well together; strawberries or raspberries and an orange-flavoured liqueur (in which case you can use the fruit raw); stewed apples and calvados or brandy; banana with rum; peaches or apricots go well with the Italian almond-flavoured liqueur Amaretto, which would also complement the flavour of the almond macaroons. For a less rich (and less fattening) dessert, natural yogurt can be used instead of the whipping cream or, for those who are not so keen on yogurt, a combination of half cream, half yogurt, which is less sharp in flavour.

Snacks and Suppers

Pizzas, quiches, soufflés, omelettes and other egg dishes, burgers, rice and pasta—these all fall into the category of 'meals in a hurry'. And with busy modern lifestyles, it is this kind of food that's wanted more and more. Don't send out for 'take-away'—your family will enjoy homemade 'fast food' much more, and you can be sure of knowing exactly what they're eating.

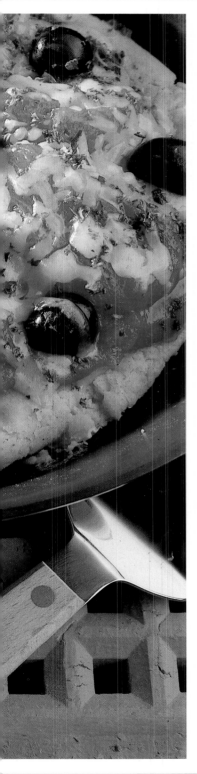

PIZZA-IN-THE-PAN ⊝ ✔

| 0.25 | £ | 1150 cals |

Serves 2

225 g (8 oz) self-raising flour

salt and freshly ground pepper

60 ml (4 tbsp) vegetable oil

60 ml (4 tbsp) water

75 ml (5 tbsp) tomato purée

397 g (14 oz) can tomatoes, drained and chopped

175 g (6 oz) Cheddar cheese, grated

chopped fresh herbs

a few black olives

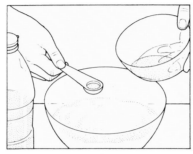

1 Sift the flour and seasoning into a bowl. Make a well in the centre and pour in 30 ml (2 tbsp) of the oil and 60 ml (4 tbsp) of the water. Mix to a soft dough—you will find that it binds together very quickly, although you may need to add a little more water.

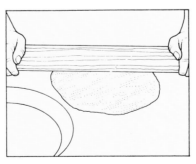

2 Knead the dough lightly on a floured surface, then roll out to a circle that will fit a medium-sized frying pan.

3 Heat half the remaining oil in the pan. Add the circle of dough and fry gently for about 5 minutes until the base is cooked and lightly browned.

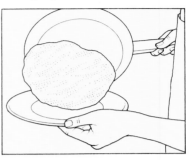

4 Turn the dough out onto a plate and flip it over.

5 Heat the remaining oil in the pan, then slide the dough back into the pan, browned side uppermost. Spread with the tomato purée, then top with the tomatoes and sprinkle over grated cheese, herbs and black olives.

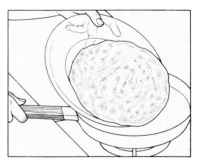

6 Cook for a further 5 minutes until the underside is done, then slide the pan under a pre-heated grill. Cook for 3–4 minutes until the cheese melts. Serve immediately.

Menu Suggestion
Serve with a mixed salad and an Italian red wine such as Chianti Classico or Valpolicella.

Tomato and Herb Quiche ⊖

| 1.00 | ✳ | 423–634 cals |

Serves 4–6

225 g (8 oz) packet frozen shortcrust
  pastry, thawed

350 g (12 oz) ripe tomatoes

3 eggs

175 g (6 oz) Caerphilly cheese,
  grated

150 ml ($\frac{1}{4}$ pint) single cream

15 ml (1 tbsp) chopped fresh herbs
  (eg sage and thyme) or 10 ml
  (2 tsp) dried mixed herbs

salt and freshly ground pepper

1 Roll out the pastry on a
  floured surface and use to line
a 23.5 cm (9 inch) flan tin or dish
placed on a baking sheet. Prick
the base with the prongs of a fork,
line with foil and baking beans and
bake blind in the oven at 200°C
(400°F) mark 6 for 15 minutes.

2 Meanwhile, skin the tomatoes.
  Put them in a heatproof bowl,
pour over boiling water and leave
to stand for 2–3 minutes. Drain,
plunge into ice-cold water, then
remove them one at a time and
peel off the skin with your fingers.

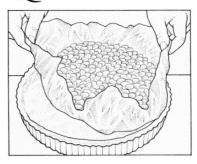

3 Remove the foil and beans
  from the pastry case and
return to the oven for 5 minutes.

4 Meanwhile, break the eggs
  into a bowl and beat lightly.
Add the cheese, cream, herbs and
seasoning to taste and beat lightly
again to mix.

5 Remove the pastry case from
  the oven. Slice the tomatoes
and arrange half of them in the
bottom of the pastry case. Slowly
pour the egg and cheese mixture
over the tomatoes, then arrange
the remaining tomato on top.

6 Bake in the oven for 20–25
  minutes until the filling is just
set. Remove and leave to stand for
15 minutes before serving.

Menu Suggestion

In late summer when tomatoes are
sweet and plentiful, this quiche
makes the perfect lunch dish
served with a fresh green salad and
a bottle of chilled dry white wine.
Cut into thin wedges to serve 8, it
also makes a delicious starter.

SURPRISE SOUFFLÉ

| 1.15 | 474 cals |

Serves 4

75 g (3 oz) butter
50 g (2 oz) flour
300 ml ($\frac{1}{2}$ pint) milk
100 g (4 oz) Gruyère cheese, grated
1.25 ml ($\frac{1}{4}$ tsp) ground mace
salt and freshly ground pepper
5 eggs, separated
**225 g (8 oz) button mushrooms,
  finely sliced**

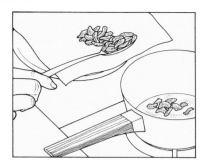

1 Melt 50 g (2 oz) of the butter in a saucepan, sprinkle in the flour and cook for 1–2 minutes, stirring constantly.

2 Remove from the heat and gradually add the milk, beating constantly after each addition. Return to the heat and bring to the boil, stirring, then lower the heat and add the cheese, mace and seasoning to taste. Simmer for about 5 minutes until the cheese melts and the sauce is very thick.

3 Remove from the heat and leave to cool for 5 minutes, then stir in the egg yolks one at a time. Set aside.

4 Melt the remaining butter in a separate pan, add the mushrooms and fry over a high heat for 2 minutes only. Remove from the pan with a slotted spoon; drain on absorbent kitchen paper.

5 Whisk the egg whites until stiff, then fold into the cheese sauce. Spoon three-quarters into a well-buttered 1.5 litre (3 pint) soufflé dish.

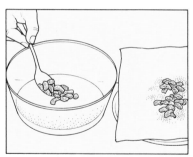

6 Make a well in the centre of the sauce, and spoon in the mushrooms. Cover with the remaining sauce. Bake in the oven at 200°C (400°F) mark 6 for 25–30 minutes until puffed up and golden on top. Serve immediately.

Menu Suggestion
Serve for a supper dish with fresh French bread and a mixed salad tossed in a vinaigrette dressing (page 151).

PEPPER AND TOMATO OMELETTE ⊖ ✎

| 0.20 | £ | 490 cals |

Serves 2

30 ml (2 tbsp) olive oil

1 onion, skinned and sliced

2 garlic cloves, skinned and crushed

1 green pepper, cored, seeded and sliced

1 red pepper, cored, seeded and sliced

4 tomatoes, skinned and sliced

5 eggs

pinch of dried mixed herbs, or to taste

salt and freshly ground pepper

50 g (2 oz) hard mature cheese (eg Parmesan, Farmhouse Cheddar), grated

1 Heat the olive oil in a non-stick frying pan. Add the onion and garlic and fry gently for 5 minutes until soft.

2 Add the pepper slices and the tomatoes and fry for a further 2–3 minutes, stirring frequently.

3 In a jug, beat the eggs lightly with the herbs and seasoning to taste. Pour into the pan, allowing the egg to run to the sides.

4 Draw in the vegetable mixture with a palette knife so that the mixture runs on to the base of the pan. Cook over moderate heat for 5 minutes until the underside of the omelette is set.

5 Sprinkle the top of the omelette with the grated cheese, then put under a pre-heated hot grill for 2–3 minutes until set and browned. Slide onto a serving plate and cut into wedges to serve.

Menu Suggestion
Pepper and Tomato Omelette can be served hot, straightaway, but it has far more flavour if left to go cold before serving. In this way, it makes the most perfect packed lunch or picnic food.

PEPPER AND TOMATO OMELETTE

This type of omelette is different from the classic French kind, which is cooked for a very short time and served folded over. Pepper and Tomato Omelette is more like the Spanish tortilla, a flat omelette which is cooked for a fairly long time so that the eggs become quite set, then browned under a hot grill so that both sides become firm. Some Spanish cooks turn their tortilla several times during cooking, and there is even a special kind of plate used in Spain which is designed to make the turning easier. Take care when making this kind of omelette that the frying pan you use is not too heavy to lift when you are transferring it to finish off the cooking under the grill. Light, non-stick frying pans are better than the traditional cast iron ones.

COCOTTE EGGS ⊝ ✐

| 0.35 | 310 cals |

Serves 4

25 g (1 oz) butter

1 small onion, skinned and finely
  chopped

4 rashers of lean back bacon,
  rinded and finely chopped

100 g (4 oz) button mushrooms,
  finely chopped

10 ml (2 tsp) tomato purée

10 ml (2 tsp) chopped fresh
  tarragon or 5 ml (1 tsp) dried
  tarragon

salt and freshly ground pepper

4 eggs, size 2

120 ml (8 tbsp) double cream

chopped fresh tarragon,
  to garnish

1 Melt the butter in a small
saucepan, add the onion and
fry gently until soft. Add the
bacon and fry until beginning to
change colour, then add the
mushrooms and tomato purée.
Continue frying for 2–3 minutes
until the juices run, stirring
constantly.

2 Remove from the heat and stir
in the tarragon and seasoning
to taste. Divide the mixture
equally between 4 cocottes,
ramekins or individual soufflé
dishes. Make a slight indentation
in the centre of each one.

3 Break an egg into each dish, on
top of the mushroom and
bacon mixture, then slowly pour
30 ml (2 tbsp) cream over each
one. Sprinkle with salt and freshly
ground pepper to taste.

4 Place the cocottes on a baking
tray and bake in the oven at
180°C (350°F) mark 4 for 10–12
minutes until the eggs are set.
Serve immediately.

Menu Suggestion
Serve for breakfast, brunch, lunch
or supper, with triangles of wholemeal or granary toast and butter.

COCOTTE EGGS

As an alternative to the
mushrooms in this recipe, you
can use fresh tomatoes. At the
end of the summer when they
are often overripe, they are best
used for cooking rather than in
salads, and this baked egg dish is
a good way to use them up. Skin
them first if you have time as this
will make the finished dish more
palatable. A quick way to skin a
few tomatoes is to pierce one at a
time with a fork in the stalk end
and then hold in the flame of a
gas hob. Turn the tomato until
the skin blisters and bursts, leave
until cool enough to handle, then
peel off the skin with your
fingers. To replace the
mushrooms, use 4 medium
tomatoes, chopped, and substitute basil for the tarragon, if
available.

MEXICAN BEEF TACOS ⊖✓

| 0.40 | ✳* | 515 cals |

* freeze chilli beef mixture after step 2

Serves 4

30 ml (2 tbsp) vegetable oil

1 onion, skinned and finely chopped

1–2 garlic cloves, skinned and crushed

5–10 ml (1–2 tsp) chilli powder, according to taste

350 g (12 oz) lean minced beef

225 g (8 oz) can tomatoes

15 ml (1 tbsp) tomato purée

2.5 ml ($\frac{1}{2}$ tsp) sugar

salt and freshly ground pepper

283 g (10 oz) can red kidney beans, drained and rinsed

8 taco shells

shredded lettuce and grated Cheddar cheese, to serve

1 Heat the oil in a pan, add the onion, garlic and chilli powder and fry gently until soft. Add the minced beef and fry until browned, stirring and pressing with a wooden spoon to remove any lumps.

2 Stir in the tomatoes with their juice and the tomato purée. Crush the tomatoes well with the spoon, then bring to the boil, stirring. Lower the heat, add the sugar and seasoning to taste, then simmer, uncovered, for 20 minutes until thick and reduced. Stir occasionally during this time to combine the ingredients and prevent them from sticking.

3 Add the kidney beans to the pan and heat through for 5 minutes. Meanwhile, heat the taco shells in the oven according to the instructions on the packet.

4 To serve, divide the meat mixture equally between the taco shells, then top with grated cheese and shredded lettuce. Eat immediately, before the taco shells soften with the heat of the beef.

Menu Suggestion

Crisp taco shells filled with spicy hot beef chilli are perfect for an impromptu snack—teenagers love them. Place warm taco shells on the table with bowls of chilli beef, cheese and lettuce and let everyone make their own. Serve with ice-cold drinks such as cola, root beer or lager.

MEXICAN BEEF TACOS

Take care when adding chilli powder, because strengths vary considerably from one brand to another. Always add the smallest amount specified, then taste before adding more. If you prefer a mild chilli flavour, buy 'chilli seasoning', which is available in small glass bottles at most supermarkets. A blend of chilli powder and other spices, it has less 'fire' than real chilli powder, and can be used in larger amounts.

Mexican taco shells are available in boxes at most large supermarkets. Some packs come with a ready-mixed sauce in a sachet, so make sure it is only the taco shells you are buying.

SAUSAGE BURGERS ⊙ ✐

| 0.50 | £ | 390 cals |

Makes 8

450 g (1 lb) pork sausagemeat

125 g (4 oz) fresh white
    breadcrumbs

1 medium onion, skinned and
    finely chopped

60 ml (4 tbsp) chopped fresh
    parsley

1 egg, size 2, beaten

salt and freshly ground pepper

60 ml (4 tbsp) flour

vegetable oil for frying

1 In a bowl or food processor,
mix together the sausagemeat,
breadcrumbs, onion, parsley, egg
and seasoning to taste.

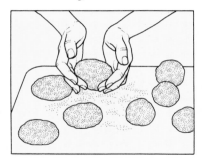

2 Divide the mixture into eight
on a floured board. With well-
floured hands, shape into rounds
about 1 cm (½ inch) thick.

3 Place the burgers on a lightly
floured plate and chill in the
refrigerator for at least 30 minutes.

4 Heat a little oil in a frying pan,
add half of the burgers and fry
for 8–10 minutes a side, turning
once only. Drain on absorbent
kitchen paper and keep hot while
frying the remainder.

Menu Suggestion
Serve fresh Sausage Burgers hot
in warmed burger baps with a
selection of pickles and ketchup.
Accompany with a mixed salad of
lettuce, tomato and cucumber.

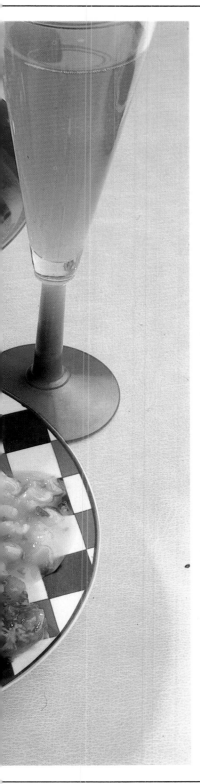

WHOLEWHEAT, APRICOT AND NUT SALAD ✓

| 0.35* | f | 325–433 cals |

* plus overnight soaking and 2 hours chilling

Serves 6–8

225 g (8 oz) wholewheat grain

3 celery sticks, washed and trimmed

125 g (4 oz) dried apricots

100 g (4 oz) Brazil nuts, roughly chopped

50 g (2 oz) unsalted peanuts

60 ml (4 tbsp) olive oil

30 ml (2 tbsp) lemon juice

salt and freshly ground pepper

chopped fresh parsley and cucumber slices, to garnish

1 Soak the wholewheat grain overnight in plenty of cold water. Drain, then tip into a large saucepan of boiling water. Simmer gently for 25 minutes or until the grains have a little bite left.

2 Drain the wholewheat into a colander and rinse under cold running water. Tip into a large serving bowl and set aside.

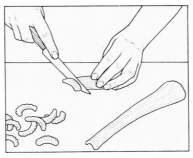

3 Cut the celery into small diagonal pieces with a sharp knife. Stir into the wholewheat.

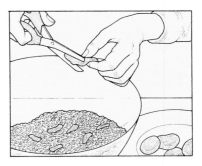

4 Using kitchen scissors, snip the apricots into small pieces over the wholewheat. Add the nuts and stir well to mix.

5 Mix the oil and lemon juice together with plenty of seasoning, pour over the salad and toss well. Chill in the refrigerator for 2 hours, then toss again and adjust seasoning just before serving.

Menu Suggestion
Serve for a healthy lunch dish with hot granary or wholemeal rolls and a green salad.

WHOLEWHEAT, APRICOT AND NUT SALAD
You can buy the wholewheat grain for this recipe in any good health food shop. Sometimes it is referred to as 'kibbled' wheat, because the grains are cracked in a machine called a 'kibbler', which breaks the grain into little pieces. Do not confuse wholewheat grain with cracked wheat (sometimes also called bulghar or burghul), which is cooked wheat which has been dried and cracked, used extensively in the cooking of the Middle East. Although different, the two kinds of wheat can be used interchangeably in most recipes.

QUICK CHICKEN AND MUSSEL PAELLA ⊖ ✎

| 0.50 | £ | 520–780 cals |

Serves 4–6

60 ml (4 tbsp) olive oil

about 450 g (1 lb) boneless chicken meat, skinned and cut into bite-sized cubes

1 onion, skinned and chopped

2 garlic cloves, skinned and crushed

1 large red pepper, cored, seeded and sliced into thin strips

3 tomatoes, skinned and chopped

400 g (14 oz) Valencia or risotto rice

1.2 litres (2¼ pints) boiling chicken stock

5 ml (1 tsp) paprika

2.5 ml (½ tsp) saffron powder

salt and freshly ground pepper

two 150 g (5 oz) jars mussels, drained

lemon wedges, peeled prawns and fresh mussels (optional), to serve

1 Heat the oil in a large, deep frying pan, add the cubes of chicken and fry over moderate heat until golden brown on all sides. Remove from the pan with a slotted spoon and set aside.

2 Add the onion, garlic and red pepper to the pan and fry gently for 5 minutes until softened. Add the tomatoes and fry for a few more minutes until the juices run, then add the rice and stir to combine with the oil and vegetables.

3 Pour in 1 litre (1¾ pints) of the boiling stock (it will bubble furiously), then add half the paprika, the saffron powder and seasoning to taste. Stir well, lower the heat and add the chicken.

4 Simmer, uncovered, for 30 minutes until the chicken is cooked through, stirring frequently during this time to prevent the rice from sticking. When the mixture becomes dry, stir in a few tablespoons of boiling stock. Repeat as often as necessary to keep the paella moist until the end of the cooking time.

5 To serve, fold in the mussels and heat through. Taste and adjust seasoning, then garnish with lemon wedges, mussels in their shells and a sprinkling of the remaining paprika.

Menu Suggestion
Serve for a substantial supper dish with fresh crusty bread and a mixed green salad.

QUICK CHICKEN AND MUSSEL PAELLA

Spain's most famous dish, paella, gets its name from the pan in which it is traditionally cooked—*paellera*. The pan is usually made of a heavy metal such as cast iron, with sloping sides and two flat handles on either side. The *paellera* is not only the best utensil for cooking paella, it is also the most attractive way to serve it, so if you like to make paella fairly frequently it is well worth investing in one—they are obtainable from specialist kitchen shops and some large hardware stores.

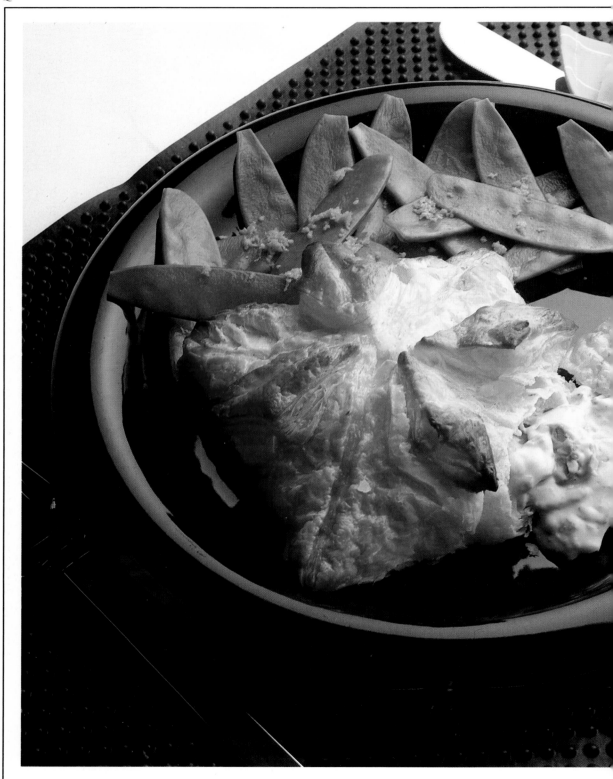

HADDOCK AND MUSHROOM PUFFS 🥄

0.40*	✳*	791 cals

* plus 30 minutes chilling; freeze at
step 5

Serves 4

397 g (14 oz) packet puff pastry, thawed if frozen
450 g (1 lb) haddock fillet, skinned
213 g (7½ oz) can creamed mushrooms
5 ml (1 tsp) lemon juice
20 ml (4 tsp) capers, chopped
15 ml (1 tbsp) snipped fresh chives or 5 ml (1 tsp) dried
salt and freshly ground pepper
1 egg

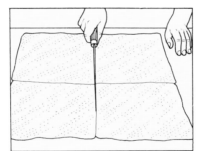

1 Roll out the pastry on a floured surface into a 40.5 cm (16 inch) square. Using a sharp knife, cut into four squares, trim the edges and reserve the trimmings of pastry.

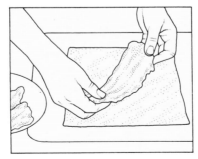

2 Place the squares on dampened baking sheets. Divide the fish into four and place diagonally across the pastry squares.

3 Combine the creamed mushrooms with the lemon juice, capers, chives and seasoning to taste. Mix well, then spoon over the pieces of haddock fillet.

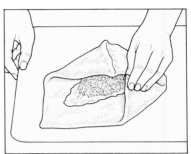

4 Brush the edges of each square lightly with water. Bring the four points of each square together and seal the edges to form an envelope-shaped parcel.

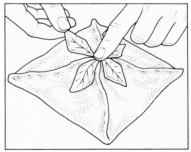

5 Decorate with pastry trimmings and make a small hole in the centre of each parcel. Chill in the refrigerator for 30 minutes.

6 Beat the egg with a pinch of salt and use to glaze the pastry. Bake in the oven at 220°C (425°F) mark 7 for about 20 minutes or until the pastry is golden brown and well risen. Serve hot.

Menu Suggestion
Serve for a substantial supper dish with a seasonal green vegetable such as French beans.

TUNA AND PASTA IN SOURED CREAM ⊖ ✔

| 0.25 | 780 cals |

Serves 4

225 g (8 oz) pasta spirals or shells

salt and freshly ground pepper

5 ml (1 tsp) vegetable oil

198 g (7 oz) can tuna, drained

4 eggs, hard-boiled and shelled

25 g (1 oz) butter

150 ml ($\frac{1}{4}$ pint) soured cream

5 ml (1 tsp) anchovy essence

30 ml (2 tbsp) malt vinegar

60 ml (4 tbsp) chopped fresh parsley

1 Cook the pasta in plenty of boiling salted water to which the oil has been added, for about 15 minutes until *al dente* (tender but firm to the bite). Drain well.

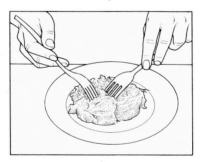

2 Meanwhile, flake the tuna fish with 2 forks. Chop the hard-boiled eggs finely.

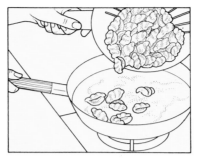

3 Melt the butter in a deep frying pan and toss in the pasta. Stir in the soured cream, anchovy essence and vinegar.

4 Add the tuna and egg to the pan with the parsley. Season well and warm through over low heat, stirring occasionally. Serve immediately.

Menu Suggestion
This rich and filling pasta dish needs a contrasting accompaniment. Serve with a crisp and crunchy green salad of chopped celery, fennel, cucumber and green pepper.

TUNA AND PASTA IN SOURED CREAM

The type of pasta you use for this dish is really a matter of personal taste, although spirals and shells are specified in the ingredients list. As long as the shapes are small (*pasta corta*), the sauce will cling to them and not slide off—Italians serve short cut pasta with fairly heavy sauces like this one which have chunks of fish or meat in them. Long pasta (*pasta lunga*) such as spaghetti and tagliatelle are best served with smoother sauces. Italian pasta in the shape of shells are called *conchiglie*, and there are many different sizes to choose from. *Farfalle* are shaped like small bow-ties; *fusilli* are spirals, so too are *spirale ricciolo*; *rotelle* are shaped like wheels. There are also many different types of short pasta shaped like macaroni—*penne* are hollow and shaped like quills with angled ends, *rigatoni* have ridges.

NOODLES IN WALNUT SAUCE

| 0.20 | 730 cals |

Serves 4

100 g (4 oz) walnut pieces

75 g (3 oz) butter, softened

1 small garlic clove, skinned and
    roughly chopped

30 ml (2 tbsp) flour

300 ml ($\frac{1}{2}$ pint) milk

275 g (10 oz) green tagliatelle

5 ml (1 tsp) vegetable oil

salt and freshly ground pepper

100 g (4 oz) Cheddar cheese,
    grated

freshly grated nutmeg

1 In a blender or food processor,
    mix together the walnuts, 50 g
(2 oz) of the butter and the garlic.
Turn into a bowl.

2 Put the remaining 25 g (1 oz)
    of butter in the blender or
food processor. Add the flour and
milk and work until evenly mixed.

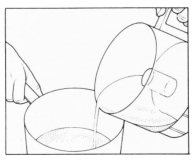

3 Turn the mixture into a sauce-
    pan and bring slowly to the
boil, stirring. Simmer 6 minutes.

4 Meanwhile, cook the tagliatelle
    in plenty of boiling salted
water, adding the oil to the water
(this prevents the pasta from sticking together).

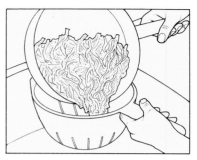

5 For the timing, follow the pack
    instructions and cook until *al
dente* (tender, but firm to the bite).
Drain the pasta thoroughly, then
return to the pan. Add the nut
butter and heat through gently,
stirring all the time.

6 Divide the pasta mixture
    equally between 4 large,
individual gratin-type dishes. Add
seasoning to the white sauce, then
use to coat the pasta.

7 Scatter the grated cheese on
    top, sprinkle with the
nutmeg, then grill for 5–10
minutes until brown and
bubbling. Serve immediately.

Menu Suggestion
Serve for a supper dish followed
by a tomato and fennel salad
dressed with olive oil, lemon juice
and chopped fresh basil.

NOODLES IN WALNUT SAUCE

Making velvety smooth sauces
is not the easiest of culinary
tasks, and most cooks seem to
have problems with them at
some time or another. Even
French chefs have been known
to sieve their sauces before
serving, to remove lumps! The
French method of cooking a roux
of butter and flour, then gradually adding milk, requires a
certain amount of skill and
judgement, whereas the all-in-
one method in this recipe is
quick and easy to do if you have
a blender or food processor—and
just about foolproof!

STUFFED BAKED POTATOES ✔

| 2.00 | £ | 362 cals |

Serves 4

4 medium potatoes, about 250 g (8 oz) each

1 medium onion, skinned

25 g (1 oz) butter or margarine

60 ml (4 tbsp) milk

125 g (4 oz) Cheddar cheese, grated

dash of Worcestershire sauce

salt and freshly ground pepper

snipped fresh chives, to garnish

1 Scrub the potatoes with a stiff vegetable brush under cold running water. Pat dry with absorbent kitchen paper and then wrap individually in foil. Bake in the oven at 200°C (400°F) mark 6 for about 1¼–1½ hours, or until just tender. Remove the potatoes from the oven, leaving the oven turned on at the same temperature.

2 Cut the potatoes in half lengthways. Scoop out most of the flesh from the insides, leaving a good rim around the edge of each potato shell. Mash the scooped-out potato in a bowl until free of lumps.

3 Finely chop the onion. Melt the fat in a small saucepan. Add the onion and fry gently until lightly browned. Add the milk and heat gently.

4 Beat this mixture into the mashed potato with half of the grated cheese, the Worcestershire sauce and seasoning to taste.

5 Spoon the potato back into the shells (or pipe with a large, star vegetable nozzle). Sprinkle over the remaining grated cheese.

6 Return to the oven for about 20 minutes, or until golden. Serve immediately, sprinkled with chives.

Menu Suggestion

Serve Stuffed Baked Potatoes on their own for a tasty snack at lunch or supper time. For a more substantial meal, serve with sausages or frankfurters.

―――――――― VARIATIONS ――――――――

Instead of the onion, cheese and Worcestershire sauce, add the following ingredients to the scooped-out mashed potato: **75 g (3 oz) bacon**, roughly chopped and fried, a little **milk, salt** and **freshly ground pepper**; or **75 g (3 oz) smoked haddock**, cooked and mashed, **5 ml (1 tsp) chopped fresh parsley**, **5 ml (1 tsp) lemon juice**, a little **milk, salt, freshly ground pepper** and **grated nutmeg**, or **30–45 ml (2–3 tbsp) cream**, **10 ml (2 tsp) snipped chives, salt**.

Pile back into potato skins and serve immediately without returning to the oven.

STUFFED BAKED POTATOES

Baked potatoes, warm and filling, are one of winter's most popular foods — and one of the easiest to cook.

For the best results, buy the varieties recommended for baking. These include Desirée, Kerrs Pink, King Edward, Majestic, Pentland Crown, Pentland Dell and Pentland Ivory. Check before buying that the potatoes are free from disease, mechanical damage and growth shoots, because many people like to eat the skin of jacket-baked potatoes, the most nutritious part. (Potatoes are a rich source of vitamin C, iron, thiamin, riboflavin and nicotinic acid, and the skins also provide dietary fibre.) Also check that the skins are not tinged with green, which is caused by exposure to light and makes the potatoes unpleasant to eat. All potatoes should be stored in the dark to prevent this problem occurring.

Teatime Treats

When time is of the essence in the kitchen, it's usually the baking that gets left out. After all, cakes and biscuits are not necessities of life, so it's easy to justify not making them. This chapter shows you just how easy it is to make cakes and other bakes in minutes rather than hours, so family and friends won't have to miss out on a few of life's little luxuries.

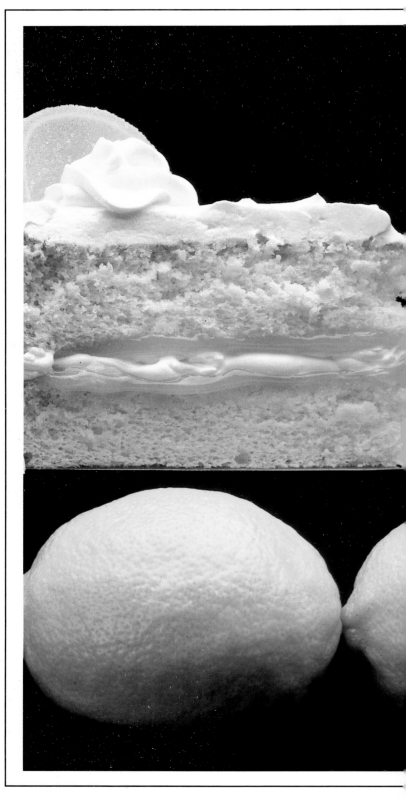

LEMON CREAM GÂTEAU ☺

| 0.50* | ✳* | 304–405 cals |

* plus 30–40 minutes cooling; freeze
without lemon decoration
Serves 6–8

100 g (4 oz) plain flour
pinch of salt
4 eggs
175 g (6 oz) caster sugar
**finely grated rind and juice of 1
  lemon**
90 ml (6 tbsp) lemon curd
100 g (4 oz) low-fat soft cheese
45 ml (3 tbsp) single cream
15 ml (1 tbsp) icing sugar
**crystallised lemon slices,
  to decorate**

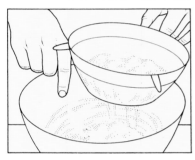

1 Sift the flour and salt into a
 bowl and set aside.

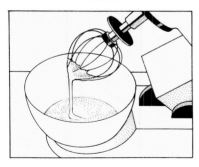

2 Beat the eggs and sugar in a
 tabletop electric mixer until
thick enough for the beaters to
leave a trail behind when lifted.

3 Fold in the sifted flour, lemon
 rind and juice; then
immediately turn into a buttered
20.5 cm (8 inch) cake tin. Bake in
the oven at 190°C (375°F) mark 5
for 20–25 minutes. Turn the cake
out onto a wire rack. Leave the
cake until completely cold, about
30–40 minutes.

4 Split the cake in half and
 spread the cut side of each half
with 45 ml (3 tbsp) lemon curd.
Whip the cheese and cream
together with the icing sugar, then
sandwich the cakes together with
about one-third of the mixture,
between the lemon curd.

5 Place the cake on a serving
 plate and swirl the remaining
cheese and cream mixture over the
top and sides. Decorate with
lemon slices and chill in the
refrigerator until serving time.

Menu Suggestion
Whisked sponges are so quick to
make once you know how, and
make perfect last-minute desserts
or coffee morning treats when
sandwiched together with yummy
fillings like this one.

**LEMON CREAM
GÂTEAU**
Making a whisked sponge in a
tabletop electric mixer is by far
the quickest and easiest method.
Whisked sponges are fatless;
they rely on lots of air to make
them light and fluffy in texture,
and beating in air is hard work
and time-consuming. Tabletop
electric mixers have heavy-
duty motors which can beat in
large amounts of air in a
relatively short time; with a
hand-held electric whisk or a
balloon whisk, you will find the
only way to incorporate so much
air is to whisk the mixture over
hot water. This is a successful
method, but it can take anything
up to 20 minutes before the
whisk leaves a ribbon trail
behind it when lifted, and then
you must continue whisking off
the heat until the mixture is cold
before folding in the flour.

SPICED WALNUT SCONES ☉ ✎

| 0.25 | £ | 123 cals |

Makes 16

125 g (4 oz) plain wholemeal flour
125 g (4 oz) plain white flour
15 ml (3 tsp) baking powder
2.5 ml (½ tsp) ground mixed spice
pinch of salt
50 g (2 oz) butter or block
    margarine
15 ml (1 tbsp) caster sugar
75 g (3 oz) walnut pieces, roughly
    chopped
10 ml (2 tsp) lemon juice
200 ml (7 fl oz) milk
honey and chopped walnuts,
    to decorate

1 Sift the flours into a bowl with the baking powder, mixed spice and salt. Stir in the bran (from the wholemeal flour) left in the bottom of the sieve. Rub in the fat. Stir in the sugar and two-thirds of the walnuts.

2 Mix the lemon juice with 170 ml (6 fl oz) of the milk and stir into the dry ingredients until evenly mixed.

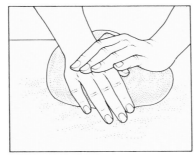

3 Turn the dough onto a floured surface and knead lightly until smooth and soft.

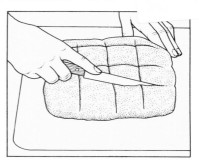

4 Roll out the dough to a 20.5 cm (8 inch) square and place on a baking sheet. Mark the surface into 16 squares, cutting the dough through to a depth of 3 mm (⅛ inch).

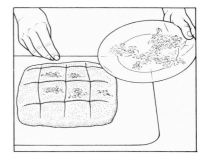

5 Lightly brush the dough with the remaining milk, then sprinkle over the remaining chopped walnut pieces.

6 Bake in the oven at 220°C (425°F) mark 7 for about 18 minutes or until well risen, golden brown and firm to the touch. Cut into squares. Serve warm, brushed with honey.

Menu Suggestion
Quick to make from store-cupboard ingredients, these Spiced Walnut Scones can be served plain or buttered, whichever you prefer.

—— VARIATION ——

For a savoury scone mixture, use **2.5 ml (½ tsp) chilli powder** instead of the sugar and omit the mixed spice.

DROP SCONES ⊖ ✒

0.20	£	55–62 cals

Makes 16–18

150 g (5 oz) self-raising flour
pinch of salt
15 ml (1 tbsp) caster sugar
15 ml (1 tbsp) vegetable oil
1 egg, beaten
150 ml ($\frac{1}{4}$ pint) milk
lard or oil, for greasing

1 Sift the flour, salt and sugar into a bowl, then add the oil, egg and milk. Stir with a wooden spoon to combine to a thick batter the consistency of double cream.

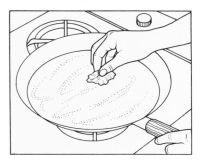

2 Grease a girdle or heavy frying pan with a little lard or oil and place over moderate heat until hot.

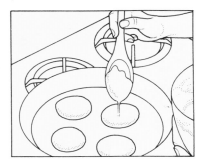

3 Drop spoonfuls of the mixture from the point of the spoon on to the pan, keeping them well apart to allow for spreading.

4 Cook over moderate heat for 2–3 minutes until bubbles rise and burst all over the surface of the scones and the undersides are golden brown. Turn them over with a palette knife and cook for 2–3 minutes on the other side.

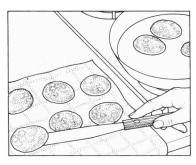

5 Transfer the cooked scones to a clean tea-towel and fold the cloth over to enclose them while making the remaining scones. Serve hot, as soon as all the scones are made.

Menu Suggestion
Made from storecupboard ingredients, Drop Scones are ideal for an impromptu tea party. Serve them with butter and jam or honey. You can also serve them for a dessert with golden or maple syrup and lashings of whipped cream!

DROP SCONES

Drop scones take their name from the fact that the mixture is 'dropped' from the mixing spoon onto the hot girdle. In the old days, they were made on the kitchen range and every cook had a girdle or griddle which was made of thick iron (an excellent conductor of heat) and had a half-hoop handle for easy lifting. Girdles can still be found in antique shops, and some kitchen specialist shops sell modern equivalents, but a heavy-based frying pan can be used with equal success.

MIXED FRUIT TEABREAD ✎

| 1.35* | ✳ | 229–287 cals |

* plus overnight soaking, 1 hour
cooling and 1–2 days maturing

Serves 8–10

175 g (6 oz) raisins

125 g (4 oz) sultanas

50 g (2 oz) currants

175 g (6 oz) soft brown sugar

300 ml ($\frac{1}{2}$ pint) strained cold tea

1 egg, beaten

225 g (8 oz) plain wholemeal flour

7.5 ml (1$\frac{1}{2}$ tsp) baking powder

2.5 ml ($\frac{1}{2}$ tsp) ground mixed spice

1 Place the dried fruit and the sugar in a large bowl. Pour over the tea, stir well to mix and leave to soak overnight.

2 The next day, add the egg, flour, baking powder and mixed spice to the fruit and tea mixture. Beat thoroughly with a wooden spoon until all the ingredients are evenly combined.

3 Spoon the cake mixture into a greased and base-lined 900 g (2 lb) loaf tin. Level the surface.

4 Bake in the oven at 180°C (350°F) mark 4 for about 1$\frac{1}{4}$ hours until the cake is well risen and a skewer inserted in the centre comes out clean.

5 Turn the cake out of the tin and leave on a wire rack until completely cold. Wrap in cling film and store in an airtight container for 1–2 days before slicing and eating.

Menu Suggestion

Serve this moist, fruity teabread sliced and buttered at teatime. Or serve with thin wedges of sharp Cheddar cheese for a snack at any time of day.

GRANDMA'S BISCUITS

| 0.35* | £ | 101 cals |

* plus cooling time

Makes 35

100 g (4 oz) butter or margarine
175 g (6 oz) dark soft brown sugar
30 ml (2 tbsp) golden syrup
150 g (5 oz) self-raising flour
2.5 ml ($\frac{1}{2}$ tsp) bicarbonate of soda
125 g (4 oz) rolled oats
150 g (5 oz) desiccated coconut
1 egg, beaten

1 Put the fat, sugar and golden syrup in a heavy-based pan and heat gently until melted, stirring occasionally.

2 Meanwhile, put the flour, bicarbonate of soda, oats and coconut in a large mixing bowl and stir well to mix.

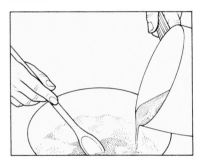

3 Pour the melted mixture on to the dry ingredients and stir well to mix. Add the beaten egg and stir again until all of the ingredients are evenly combined.

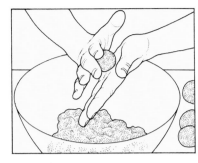

4 With the palms of your hands, shape and roll the mixture into about 35 small, walnut-sized balls.

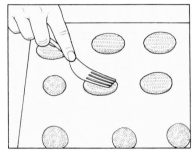

5 Place the balls slightly apart on greased baking sheets to allow for spreading during baking, then flatten with the back of a fork to make an attractive pattern.

6 Bake in the oven at 180°C (350°F) mark 4 for 12–15 minutes until browned. Leave to settle on the baking sheets for a few minutes, then transfer to a wire rack and leave to cool completely before serving. To keep crisp, store in an airtight tin.

Menu Suggestion
Crisp, crunchy and wholesome, these old-fashioned biscuits are a great hit with children—ideal for packed lunches.

CHEWY CHOCOLATE BROWNIES ⊝ ✒

0.15* | 156 cals

* plus cooling time

Makes 16

75 g (3 oz) plain flour

175 g (6 oz) dark soft brown sugar

25 g (1 oz) cocoa powder

1.25 ml ($\frac{1}{4}$ tsp) salt

100 g (4 oz) butter or margarine

2 eggs, beaten

5 ml (1 tsp) vanilla flavouring

75 g (3 oz) chopped mixed nuts

1 Put all the ingredients in a bowl and beat thoroughly (preferably with an electric whisk) until evenly combined.

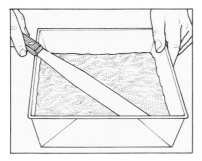

2 Turn the mixture into a greased 20.5 cm (8 inch) square cake tin and level the surface with a palette knife.

3 Bake in the oven at 180°C (350°F) mark 4 for 25 minutes until only just set (the mixture should still wobble slightly in the centre). Stand the cake tin on a wire rack and leave until the cake is completely cold. Cut into 16 squares and put in an airtight tin.

Menu Suggestion

Moist and munchy Chocolate Brownies are a favourite at any time of day. Try them as a fun dessert for children with scoops of vanilla ice cream and chocolate sauce or chopped nuts.

REFRIGERATOR COOKIES ✓

0.35* | 37–49 cals

* plus overnight chilling and about 30
minutes cooling; freeze dough at the
end of step 3

Makes 50–60

225 g (8 oz) plain flour
5 ml (1 tsp) baking powder
100 g (4 oz) butter or margarine
175 g (6 oz) caster sugar
5 ml (1 tsp) vanilla flavouring
1 egg, beaten

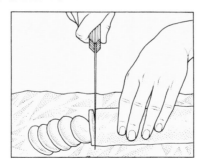

4 To shape and bake: slice the
roll very thinly into as many
cookies as required. (The remainder of the roll can be wrapped
again in the foil and returned to
the refrigerator for up to 1 week.)

5 Place the cookies well apart on
a buttered baking sheet. Bake in
the oven at 190°C (375°F) mark 5
for 10–12 minutes until golden.

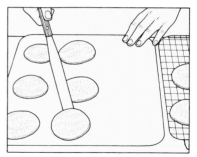

6 Leave the cookies to settle on
the baking sheet for a few
minutes, then transfer to a wire
rack and leave to cool completely.
Store in an airtight tin if not eating immediately.

Menu Suggestion
Serve for children's teas or when
unexpected visitors call. Keep a
roll of dough in the refrigerator
ready to make a batch of cookies at
a moment's notice.

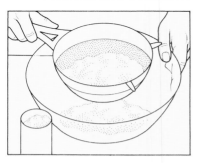

1 Sift the flour and baking
powder into a bowl. Rub in
the fat until the mixture resembles
breadcrumbs, then add the sugar
and stir until evenly combined.

2 Add the vanilla flavouring and
egg and mix to a smooth
dough with a wooden spoon.

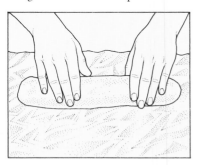

3 Turn the dough onto a large
sheet of foil and shape into a
long roll about 5 cm (2 inches) in
diameter. Wrap in the foil and
chill in the refrigerator overnight.

— VARIATIONS —

Walnut: add **50 g (2 oz) very
finely chopped walnuts** with the
sugar in step 1.
Coconut: add **50 g (2 oz)
desiccated coconut** with the
sugar in step 1.
Sultana: add **50 g (2 oz) very
finely chopped sultanas** with
the sugar in step 1.
Chocolate: add **50 g (2 oz) very
finely grated plain chocolate**
with the sugar in step 1.
Spicy: omit the vanilla and sift in
10 ml (2 tsp) ground mixed

spice with the flour in step 1.
Lemon: omit the vanilla and add
the **finely grated rind of 1
lemon** with the sugar in step 1.
Ginger: omit the vanilla and sift in
7.5 ml ($1\frac{1}{2}$ tsp) ground ginger
with the flour in step 1.
Cherry: add **50 g (2 oz) very
finely chopped glacé cherries**
with the sugar in step 1.
Orange: omit the vanilla and add
the **finely grated rind of 1
orange** with the sugar in step 1.

BROWN SODA BREAD ☉✏

0.20*	3650 cals

* plus 30 minutes cooling

Serves 6

600 g (1¼ lb) plain wholewheat flour

350 g (12 oz) plain white flour

10 ml (2 tsp) bicarbonate of soda

20 ml (4 tsp) cream of tartar

10 ml (2 tsp) salt

10 ml (2 tsp) sugar (optional)

900 ml (1½ pints) milk and water, mixed

1 Sift the flours, bicarbonate of soda, cream of tartar and salt into a bowl. Stir in the bran (from the wholewheat flour) left in the bottom of the sieve, then the sugar. Add enough milk and water to mix to a soft dough.

2 Turn the dough onto a floured surface and knead lightly until smooth and soft.

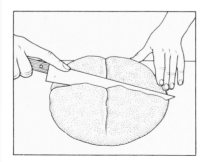

3 Shape the dough into a round. Score into quarters with a sharp knife and place on a greased baking sheet or tray.

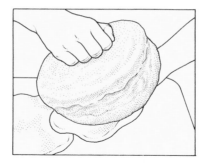

4 Bake in the oven at 220°C (425°F) mark 7 for 25–30 minutes until the bottom of the bread sounds hollow when tapped with the knuckles of your hand. Cool on a wire rack before serving.

Menu Suggestion
Soda bread is best eaten really fresh — on the day of baking. Serve with a mature Farmhouse Cheddar, tomatoes and spring onions for a homemade 'ploughman's lunch'.

BROWN SODA BREAD
Soda bread is the ideal bread to make when you are short of time for baking. The raising agent in soda bread is bicarbonate of soda mixed with an acid, which releases the carbon dioxide necessary to make the bread light. In this recipe, fresh milk is made sour (acid) with cream of tartar, but you can use bicarbonate of soda on its own with sour milk or buttermilk, which will provide enough acid without the cream of tartar. The end result is much the same whichever ingredients you use, although bread made with buttermilk does tend to have a softer texture.

Drinks Party

The quickest and easiest way to entertain a crowd is to throw a drinks party, keeping the mood informal and the food simple. To serve 15–20 people, make all 3 dips suggested here, or choose 1 or 2 and increase the quantities accordingly. Serve with sticks of raw vegetables, small crackers and Italian grissini. Make double the quantity of Asparagus Tranches and Smoked Salmon and Cheese Tartlets, but only a single quantity of the Golden Fish Nuggets. The Hot Party Punch should be sufficient to serve 15–20, but make extra if you are unsure of your guests' drinking habits!

AVOCADO AND BLUE CHEESE DIP

| 0.20 | 1842 cals | ⊝ | ✎ |

175 g (6 oz) blue cheese (eg Stilton, Gorgonzola or Dolcelatte, to taste)

300 ml (½ pint) soured cream

2 ripe avocados

juice of ½ lemon

salt and freshly ground pepper

a few slices of avocado, to garnish (optional)

1 Crumble the cheese into a bowl and mash with a fork until smooth and creamy.

2 Work the soured cream gradually into the cheese until it is evenly incorporated.

3 Cut the avocados in half and remove the stones. With a teaspoon, scoop the flesh out of the skins into a separate bowl.

4 Add the lemon juice and mash the flesh quickly with a fork. Stir the mashed avocado flesh into the cheese and cream mixture, then add seasoning to taste and stir again.

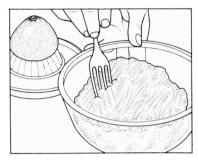

5 Cover tightly with cling film and chill in the refrigerator until serving time. (Do not prepare more than 2 hours in advance or the avocado flesh will discolour and spoil the appearance of the dip.)

6 Spoon the dip into serving bowls. Garnish with avocado slices, if liked, and serve immediately.

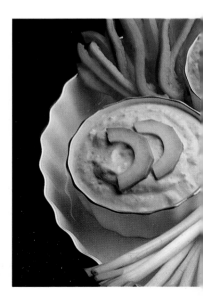

CREAMY FISH DIP ⊝✓

0.20	£ £ ✳*	4123 cals

* freeze at the end of step 2

two 198 g (7 oz) cans crab meat

two 198 g (7 oz) cans shrimps

450 g (1 lb) full-fat soft cheese

60 ml (4 tbsp) creamed horseradish

finely grated rind and juice of 1 lemon

5 ml (1 tsp) paprika

freshly ground pepper

lemon slices, to garnish

1 Drain the crab meat and shrimps and put the flesh in an electric blender or food processor. Work until the flesh is broken down to a pulp.

2 Add the cheese in batches and work until evenly combined with the fish. When all the cheese is incorporated, work in the creamed horseradish, lemon rind and juice, paprika and pepper.

3 Turn the mixture into serving bowls and grind black pepper liberally over the surface. Garnish with lemon slices and chill in the refrigerator until serving time.

HOT PARTY PUNCH ⊝✓

0.35	131–175 cals

Makes 4.8 litres (8 pints)

12 cloves

2 oranges

4.8 litres (8 pints) dry cider

100 g (4 oz) sugar

175 ml (6 fl oz) brandy

pinch of ground cinnamon

pinch of ground ginger

2 red-skinned dessert apples

1 Press the cloves into the whole oranges and place in a large saucepan. Pour in the cider and sugar and heat gently until simmering, stirring occasionally.

2 Stir in the brandy and spices, then simmer for 20 minutes.

3 To serve, core and slice the apples (but do not peel them). Pour the punch into a warmed bowl and float the apple slices on the top. Ladle into individual glasses as required.

HOT TOMATO DIP ⊝✓

0.30*	3231 cals

* plus cooling time

45 ml (3 tbsp) vegetable oil

1 large onion, skinned and finely chopped

2 garlic cloves, skinned and crushed

2.5 ml ($\frac{1}{2}$ tsp) chilli powder

450 g (1 lb) ripe tomatoes, skinned and chopped

300 ml ($\frac{1}{2}$ pint) thick homemade mayonnaise (see page 151)

dash of Tabasco sauce, to taste

salt and freshly ground pepper

1 Heat the oil in a heavy-based saucepan, add the onion and garlic and fry gently for about 5 minutes until almost soft.

2 Add the chilli powder and fry for 1–2 minutes, stirring constantly, to prevent it from burning. Add the tomatoes and stir well with a wooden spoon to break them up. Add seasoning to taste and bring to the boil, then lower the heat and simmer, uncovered, for 20 minutes until thick. Remove from the heat and leave until completely cold.

3 Turn the tomato sauce into a bowl and stir in the mayonnaise. Add Tabasco to taste. Stir well to mix, then taste and adjust the seasoning. Spoon the mixture into serving bowls, cover with cling film and chill in the refrigerator until serving time.

ASPARAGUS TRANCHES ⊖

| 0.40* | 72 cals |

* plus 30 minutes cooling

Makes 24

12 spears fresh asparagus, trimmed, or 283 g (10 oz) can asparagus tips, drained

salt and freshly ground pepper

212 g (7½ oz) packet frozen puff pastry, thawed

60 ml (4 tbsp) thick mayonnaise

2.5 ml (½ tsp) lemon juice

25 g (1 oz) walnuts, finely chopped

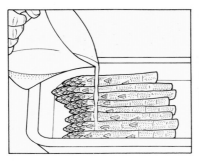

1 Place the asparagus in a large roasting tin. Cover with water and add a good pinch of salt.

2 Bring the water to the boil, then simmer until the asparagus is just tender. Remove and drain.

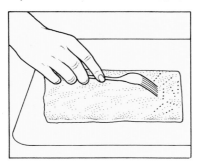

3 Roll the pastry out on a lightly floured surface to a 40.5 × 15 cm (16 × 6 inch) rectangle. Cut this in two to make 2 smaller rectangles, each measuring 20.5 × 15 cm (8 × 6 inches). Place on a wetted baking sheet. Prick all over.

4 Bake the tranches in the oven at 200°C (400°F) mark 6 for 10–15 minutes or until puffed up and golden. Transfer very carefully to a wire rack and leave to cool (about 30 minutes).

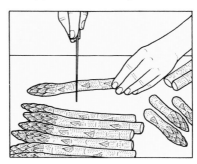

5 Cut the asparagus into 5 cm (2 inch) lengths, measuring from the tip. If using thick fresh asparagus, halve each tip lengthwise. Put the off-cuts in a blender or food processor with the mayonnaise, lemon juice and seasoning and work together until evenly combined.

6 Not more than 30 minutes before serving, trim the pastry rectangles neatly with a sharp knife to 15 × 10 cm (6 × 4 inches).

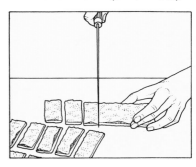

7 Spread the asparagus mayonnaise evenly over the surface of the pastry. Cut into 24 fingers, each 5 cm × 2.5 cm (2 × 1 inch). Arrange an asparagus tip on each finger, and sprinkle with the chopped walnuts.

SMOKED SALMON AND CHEESE TARTLETS

0.40*	£	101 cals

* plus 30 minutes cooling

Makes 30 tartlets

368 g (13 oz) packet frozen
   shortcrust pastry, thawed
175 g (6 oz) packet soft cheese with
   chopped chives
1 egg, beaten
150 ml ($\frac{1}{4}$ pint) single cream
100 g (4 oz) smoked salmon
   trimmings
freshly ground pepper
about 50 g (2 oz) grated Parmesan
slices of radish and strips of
   canned pimento and anchovy
   fillets, to garnish

4 Divide the filling equally
between the tartlet cases and
sprinkle with Parmesan cheese.
Bake in the oven at 180°C (350°F)
mark 4 for about 15 minutes or
until the custard mixture is set.

5 Transfer the tartlet cases to a
wire rack and leave to cool for
30 minutes. Garnish with radish
slices and strips of pimento and
anchovy before serving.

1 Roll out the pastry on a
floured surface and cut 30
rounds each 6.5 cm (2½ inch). Put
these in greased patty tins. Bake
blind for about 10 minutes.

2 Put the cheese in a bowl and
gradually beat in the egg and
cream until the mixture is smooth.

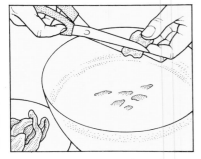

3 Snip the smoked salmon in
small pieces into the cheese
mixture. Add pepper to taste.

GOLDEN FISH NUGGETS WITH GARLIC DIP

0.45	1967 cals

Makes about 30

450 g (1 lb) monkfish
120 ml (8 tbsp) dried breadcrumbs
60 ml (4 tbsp) sesame seeds
30 ml (2 tbsp) flour
salt and freshly ground pepper
15 ml (1 tbsp) paprika
1 egg, size 2, beaten
45 ml (3 tbsp) snipped fresh chives
   or 15 ml (3 tsp) dried
1 garlic clove, skinned and crushed
300 ml (½ pint) soured cream
vegetable oil, for deep-frying
snipped fresh chives, to garnish

1 Skin the monkfish and cut into
2.5 cm (1 inch) pieces.
Combine the breadcrumbs and
sesame seeds.

––––––––– VARIATION –––––––––

Use **sliced chicken breasts**
instead of the fish, crumbed and
fried in the same way. Instead of
the garlic dip, serve them with a
raita sauce made from **chopped
fresh mint, coriander, natural
yogurt, cucumber** and **garlic**.

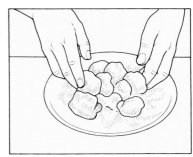

2 Toss the fish in the flour
seasoned with salt and pepper
to taste and the paprika. Dip in
the beaten egg and finely coat in
the breadcrumb and sesame seed
mixture. Chill in the refrigerator
for at least 30 minutes to set the
breadcrumb and sesame coating.

3 Combine the chives with
crushed garlic and soured
cream. Chill until serving time.

4 Heat the oil in a deep-fat frier
to 180°C (350°F) and deep-fry
the nuggets of fish for 3–4
minutes until golden. Drain well
on absorbent kitchen paper. Serve
hot, with the garlic dip.

Sunday Lunch

Entertaining on Sunday should be a relaxed affair, whether for family or friends, and this lunch menu for 6 people has been devised to be just that. The Watercress and Orange Soup can be prepared up to the reheating stage the day before, and the accompanying rolls can be made in less than an hour while the pork is roasting. Potatoes can be roasted with the pork, and the Crunchy Cabbage accompaniment takes only 15 minutes to prepare and cook. And for dessert, there's a good old-fashioned crumble, which can be prepared the night before, then popped into the oven when the main course is served.

WATERCRESS AND ORANGE SOUP

| 0.45 | ✳ | 140 cals |

Serves 6

2 large bunches watercress, trimmed and washed
50 g (2 oz) butter or margarine
2 medium onions, roughly chopped
45 ml (3 tbsp) flour
1.1 litres (2 pints) chicken stock
salt and freshly ground pepper
finely grated rind and juice of 1 orange
150 ml (¼ pint) single cream (optional)
few slices of orange, to garnish

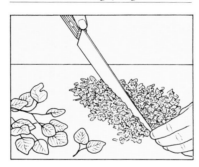

1 Reserve a few sprigs of watercress for the garnish, then chop the rest.

2 Melt the fat in a large saucepan. Add the chopped watercress and onions, cover and cook gently for 10–15 minutes.

3 Remove the pan from the heat and stir in the flour, stock and seasoning. Bring slowly to the boil, stirring all the time. Cover and simmer gently for 30 minutes. Stir in the orange rind and juice.

4 Leave to cool a little, then purée in an electric blender or food processor.

5 Return the soup to the rinsed-out pan and reheat. Stir in the single cream (if using) and heat through. (Do not boil or the soup will curdle.) Adjust the seasoning. Serve garnished with orange slices and watercress sprigs.

VARIATION

If preferred, this soup can be served chilled. Do not reheat as in step 5, simply stir in half of the single cream after the soup has gone cold. Chill in the refrigerator for at least 2 hours before serving, then swirl in the remaining cream just before serving.

POPPYSEED ROLLS ✓

| 0.55* | £ | ✳ | 88 cals |

* plus 20 minutes cooling
Makes 12 rolls

280 g (10 oz) white bread mix
450 ml (3 tbsp) poppyseeds
200 ml (7 fl oz) warm milk
beaten egg and milk, mixed,
  to glaze

1 Empty the bread mix into a bowl, add 30 ml (2 tbsp) of the poppyseeds and stir well to mix.

2 Add the warm milk and mix well with a wooden spoon to form a firm dough.

3 Turn the dough onto a floured surface and knead according to packet instructions until smooth.

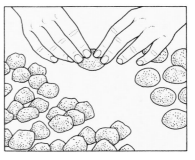

4 Cut the dough into 36 equal pieces. Shape each piece into a ball with your hands.

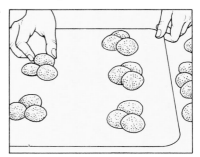

5 Sprinkle 2 baking sheets with flour, then place the dough balls on the sheets, in triangular groups of three. Leave to rise in a warm place for 10 minutes.

6 Brush the rolls with the beaten egg and milk mixture and then sprinkle with the remaining poppyseeds.

7 Bake in the oven at 200°C (400°F) mark 6 for about 20 minutes until golden. Cool the rolls for about 20 minutes on a wire rack before serving.

FRENCH PORK IN WINE ⊖

| 3.30 | £ £ | 982 cals |

Serves 6

2 kg (4½ lb) loin of pork, boned
salt and freshly ground pepper
3 garlic cloves, skinned
few fresh or dried sage sprigs
30 ml (2 tbsp) olive oil
25 g (1 oz) butter
300 ml (½ pint) dry white wine
30 ml (2 tbsp) redcurrant jelly
fresh sage leaves, to garnish

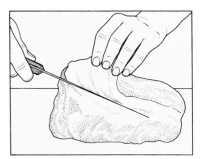

1 Lay the joint of pork out flat on a board and cut off the skin and fat with a sharp knife.

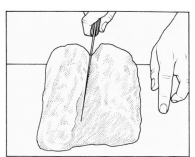

2 With a sharp, pointed knife, make a shallow cut along the length of the inside of the meat (this will make it easier to roll). Sprinkle the meat liberally with salt and pepper.

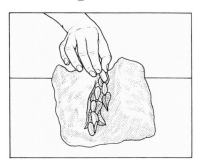

3 Cut each garlic clove into 3–4 slivers, then place at regular intervals along the length of the meat with the sprigs of sage.

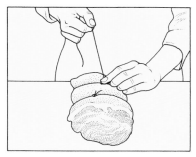

4 Roll the meat up lengthways and tie at regular intervals with string. Heat the oil and butter in a large flameproof casserole into which the pork just fits. Put the pork in the casserole and lightly brown on all sides.

5 Pour in the wine and bring slowly to the boil, then cover and cook in the oven at 170°C (325°F) mark 3 for 3 hours until tender, basting occasionally.

6 To serve, remove the pork from the casserole and set aside in a warm place to settle for 15 minutes before carving. Stir the redcurrant jelly into the cooking liquid and boil rapidly to reduce.

7 Remove the string from the pork and place the joint on a warmed serving platter. Drizzle a little sauce over the pork and garnish with fresh sage leaves.

CRUNCHY CABBAGE ⊖ 🥄

| 0.15 | £ | ✳ | 95 cals |

Serves 6

350 g (12 oz) red cabbage

225 g (8 oz) cooked beetroot, skinned

1 medium onion, skinned and thinly sliced

about 30 ml (2 tbsp) peanut or vegetable oil

30 ml (2 tbsp) creamed horseradish

salt and freshly ground pepper

1 Finely shred the red cabbage, discarding the core and any thick, woody stalks.

2 Grate the beetroot on the coarse side of a conical or box grater or, if preferred, chop finely.

3 Heat 30 ml (2 tbsp) oil in a wok or large frying pan until smoking. Stir in the cabbage and onion. Cook over high heat for 3–4 minutes, stirring all the time, until the cabbage has softened a little but still retains its crispness. Add a little more oil if necessary.

4 Stir in the beetroot, horse-radish and seasoning to taste. Cook, stirring, for a further few minutes to heat through. Serve immediately.

SHERRIED PLUM CRUMBLE ⊖ 🥄

| 0.45 | 282 cals |

Serves 6

397 g (14 oz) can red plums

30 ml (2 tbsp) sherry

100 g (4 oz) flour

50 g (2 oz) butter or margarine

25 g (1 oz) chopped almonds

50 g (2 oz) demerara sugar

fresh pouring cream, natural yogurt or soured cream, to serve

1 Strain the plums and remove the stones. Divide the plums equally between four small soufflé dishes and sprinkle a little sherry over each.

2 Make the crumble topping. Sift the flour into a bowl, then rub in the fat until the mixture resembles fine breadcrumbs. Stir in the almonds and sugar. Sprinkle evenly over the plums.

3 Bake in the oven at 190°C (375°F) mark 5 for about 30 minutes until golden brown on top. Serve hot, with cream, yogurt or soured cream.

119

Easy Barbecue

Barbecues are a boon for busy people who like to entertain, because the cooking has to be left until the guests arrive! This barbecue menu for 8 people is suitable for a daytime or evening barbecue. Make the salads several hours in advance or even the night before, and leave the drumsticks and kebabs to marinate overnight. The tropical sauce for the bananas can be made several hours ahead, which just leaves the fruit cup to make as guests arrive. Nothing could be more simple.

BULGAR WHEAT SALAD ⊖ ✎

| 0.15* | 340 cals |

* plus 30 minutes soaking

Serves 8

350 g (12 oz) bulgar wheat (cracked wheat)
1 medium cucumber, chopped
175 g (6 oz) walnuts, chopped
60 ml (4 tbsp) chopped fresh dill
90 ml (6 tbsp) sunflower oil
45 ml (3 tbsp) white wine vinegar
1 garlic clove, skinned and crushed
salt and freshly ground pepper
lettuce leaves and sprigs of dill, to serve

1 Put the bulgar wheat in a bowl, pour in enough cold water to cover and then leave to soak for 30 minutes.

2 Squeeze the wheat dry with your hands, then put in a large bowl with the cucumber, walnuts and dill. Mix together well.

3 Make the dressing. Put the sunflower oil, wine vinegar, garlic and seasoning to taste in a separate bowl and whisk together until well emulsified.

4 Pour the dressing over the salad and toss well to combine. Pile onto lettuce leaves to serve, and garnish with dill sprigs.

HONEY BARBECUED DRUMSTICKS ⊖ 🥄

0.25* f ✳* | 243 cals

* plus 1–2 hours marinating; freeze
in the marinade

Serves 8

60 ml (4 tbsp) clear honey
grated rind and juice of 2 lemons
grated rind and juice of 2 oranges
90 ml (6 tbsp) soy sauce
2.5 ml ($\frac{1}{2}$ tsp) ground coriander
salt and freshly ground pepper
16 chicken drumsticks, skinned

1 Mix together the honey, lemon rind and juice, orange rind and juice, soy sauce and coriander.

2 Score the drumsticks with a sharp knife, lay in a shallow dish, and pour over the honey marinade. Cover and marinate in the refrigerator for 1–2 hours, turning the chicken occasionally during this time.

3 Cook the drumsticks on a preheated barbecue for 15–20 minutes, or until tender, turning frequently and basting with the honey marinade. Serve hot.

SAUSAGE KEBABS

0.25*	294 cals

* plus 1–2 hours marinating

Serves 8

8 rashers streaky bacon

24 cocktail sausages

24 cherry tomatoes or 6 small
   tomatoes, quartered

24 silverskin onions, well drained

90 ml (6 tbsp) vegetable oil

45 ml (3 tbsp) lemon juice

15 ml (1 tbsp) French mustard

10 ml (2 tsp) Worcestershire sauce

salt and freshly ground pepper

1 Remove the rind from the
bacon and cut each rasher into
3 pieces with sharp kitchen scissors.

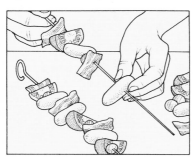

2 Thread 3 pieces of bacon on to
each of 8 oiled kebab skewers,
with 3 cocktail sausages, 3 tomatoes,
or tomato quarters and 3 onions.

3 Make the marinade. Whisk
together the oil, lemon juice,
mustard and Worcestershire
sauce. Add seasoning to taste.
Brush over the kebabs.

4 Leave the kebabs to marinate
in the refrigerator for 1–2
hours, brushing them with any
marinade that collects under them.

5 Cook the kebabs on a pre-
heated barbecue for about 10
minutes until the sausages and
bacon are cooked. Turn the
skewers often and brush with any
remaining marinade. Serve hot.

RICE SALAD RING

0.30*	160 cals	

* plus at least 1 hour chilling

Serves 8

225 g (8 oz) long grain rice

salt and freshly ground pepper

1 green pepper, seeded and diced

3 caps canned pimento, diced

198 g (7 oz) canned sweetcorn,
   drained

75 ml (5 tbsp) chopped fresh
   parsley

50 g (2 oz) salted peanuts

45 ml (3 tbsp) lemon juice

celery salt

watercress, to garnish

1 Cook the rice in plenty of boiling salted water for 10–15
minutes until tender, then tip into
a sieve and drain.

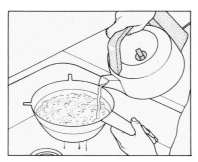

2 Rinse the rice through with
hot water from the kettle, then
rinse under cold running water
and drain thoroughly. Leave to
cool completely.

3 Blanch the green pepper
in boiling water for 1 minute,
drain, rinse under cold running
water and drain again.

4 In a large bowl, mix the cold
rice, pepper and pimento,
sweetcorn, parsley, peanuts and
lemon juice, and season well with
celery salt and pepper.

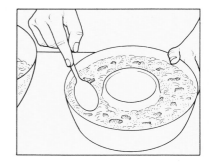

5 Press the salad into a lightly
oiled 1.4 litre (2½ pint) ring
mould and refrigerate for 1 hour.

6 Turn the rice salad ring out on
to a flat serving plate and fill
with watercress. Serve chilled.

SPARKLING FRUIT CUP ⊝ ✔

| 0.05 | £ £ | 230 cals |

Makes 3.4 litres (8 pints)

½ bottle (350 ml/12 fl oz) orange-
    flavoured liqueur

4 × 75 cl (1¼ pint) bottles
    sparkling cider

ice cubes

350 g (12 oz) fresh or frozen
    raspberries, defrosted

fresh mint sprigs

1 Make this drink up just as the guests arrive. Pour half of the liqueur into a cold glass bowl. Pour in half the wine and cider and stir quickly with a ladle.

2 Drop a few ice cubes into the bowl, then float half of the raspberries and mint sprigs on the top. Ladle into glasses immediately.

3 Make up more with the remaining ingredients as soon as the bowl needs replenishing.

BARBECUED BANANAS WITH TROPICAL SAUCE ⊝ ✔

| 0.20 | 195 cals |

Serves 8

25 g (1 oz) unsalted butter

30 ml (2 tbsp) clear honey

150 ml (¼ pint) dark rum

150 ml (¼ pint) freshly squeezed
    orange juice

150 ml (¼ pint) pineapple juice

1.25 ml (¼ tsp) ground ginger

1.25 ml (¼ tsp) ground cinnamon

8 firm, ripe bananas

blanched orange shreds,
    to decorate

pouring cream or scoops of vanilla
    ice cream, to serve (optional)

1 Make the tropical sauce. Melt the butter in a heavy-based pan, add the honey and stir until melted. Stir in the rum, orange and pineapple juices, then add the spices.

2 Bring to the boil, stirring, then simmer for a few minutes to allow the flavours to mingle. Pour into a heatproof jug and stand on the barbecue grid to keep warm.

3 When the barbecue coals are just dying down, place the bananas (in their skins) on the barbecue grid. Cook for 7 minutes, turning once, until the skins become quite black.

4 To serve, peel off the banana skins and place the bananas in a warmed serving dish. Pour over the sauce and sprinkle with orange shreds. Serve immediately, with cream or vanilla ice cream handed separately, if liked.

Informal Party

Fondue parties are great fun for an informal get-together, so why not try this more unusual idea? Cooking with a Chinese fire pot is similar to a fondue, except that the ingredients are far more varied and exotic — steak, prawns and chicken, with bean curd, rice noodles and crunchy raw vegetables, which guests cook themselves in a pot of chicken stock. For this kind of informal meal, it is perfectly acceptable to skip the starter and launch straight into the main course, which tastes good served with chilled dry white wine. For dessert, make an exotic fresh fruit salad and include lychees, mango, kiwi fruit and mandarins.

MONGOLIAN HOT POT

| 0.45* | £ £ | 482 cals |

* plus cooking time

Serves 6

450 g (1 lb) fillet steak

3 boneless chicken breasts, skinned

225 g (8 oz) bean curd (tofu)

12 jumbo (Mediterranean or Dublin Bay) prawns

225 g (8 oz) mange-touts

225 g (8 oz) broccoli spears

225 g (8 oz) young spinach leaves

225 g (8 oz) button mushrooms

225 g (8 oz) transparent rice noodles

180 ml (12 tbsp) light soy sauce

30 ml (2 tbsp) finely chopped fresh ginger

5–10 ml (1–2 tsp) hot chilli sauce, to taste

2.4 litres (4 pints) boiling chicken stock

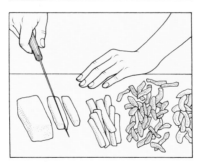

1 Cut the steak, chicken and bean curd into thin strips about 5 cm (2 inches) long.

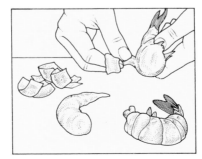

2 Peel the shells off the jumbo prawns with your fingers. Discard the shells.

3 Top and tail the mange-touts. Separate the broccoli spears into tiny sprigs or florets.

4 Arrange equal quantities of steak, chicken, bean curd, prawns, vegetables and noodles on each of 6 individual serving plates. Cover with cling film and leave in a cold place until serving time.

5 Mix half the soy sauce with the fresh ginger and half with the chilli sauce. Put 15 ml (1 tbsp) of each sauce in each of 6 tiny Chinese bowls or saucers.

6 To serve, pour the boiling stock into a Chinese fire pot standing over a charcoal burner (or into a fondue pot placed over a spirit burner) standing in the centre of the dining table. Place a plate of prepared ingredients for each guest, 2 bowls or saucers of dipping sauce (1 of each flavour) and chopsticks. Let the guests pick up the raw ingredients with chopsticks and cook them for themselves in the boiling stock, starting with the noodles, using them as a base. They then dip the cooked food in the sauces before eating. When all the ingredients have been cooked and eaten, ladle the stock into soup bowls and serve as a finish to the meal.

MONGOLIAN HOT POT

The fire pot used to cook this unusual meal was introduced to the Chinese by the Mongols when they invaded China during the fourteenth century. It works on the same principle as the Swiss fondue pot, which you can use instead if you have one.

Transparent rice noodles are available at oriental stores, sometimes called mung bean threads because they are made from mung bean flour. Soak them in water for 10 minutes before you use them.

Brunch Party

A brunch party for 8 people is a wonderful idea for weekend entertaining, and far more relaxing than a dinner party, for both guests and hosts alike.

The brunch idea is popular in America, especially in big cities where it is often served in restaurants and bars on Sundays. Simply offer each guest a glass of Champagne Cocktail as soon as they arrive, then let them help themselves to the food.

CHAMPAGNE COCKTAIL ⊝ 🥄

| 0.05 | £ £ | 151 cals |

Makes 8

8 sugar lumps

120 ml (8 tbsp) peach or apricot brandy

1 bottle champagne, well chilled

8 strips of thinly pared orange rind or 8 orange slices (optional)

1 Put a sugar lump in the bottom of each of 8 champagne glasses. Pour 15 ml (1 tbsp) of brandy into each glass and leave to soak for a few minutes.

2 Open the champagne and pour into the glasses straightaway. Serve immediately, each glass garnished with an orange twist or orange slice, if liked.

———— VARIATION ————

If liked, a few drops of **Angostura bitters** may be sprinkled over the sugar lumps before the brandy.

BAGELS WITH SMOKED SALMON AND CREAM CHEESE ⊖ ✎

| 0.30 | £ £ | 1458 cals |

Serves 8

225 g (8 oz) packet unsalted butter, chilled

12 bagels

700 g (1½ lb) cream cheese

24 thin slices smoked salmon

freshly ground black pepper

lemon wedges, to serve

1 Make butter curls. Draw a butter curler towards you along the length of the block of butter. Pile the curls up as you make them in a chilled serving bowl. Chill in the refrigerator until serving time.

2 Warm the bagels through in the oven at 170°C (325°F) mark 3 for 10 minutes.

3 Meanwhile, put the cream cheese in 1 or 2 serving bowls. Arrange the smoked salmon slices attractively on a wooden board, grind a little black pepper on top. Garnish with lemon wedges.

4 Split each bagel in half cross-ways and place in a napkin-lined basket. Serve immediately, while still warm. Guests help themselves—spreading bagels with butter and cream cheese, topping each one with a slice of salmon and a squeeze of lemon.

RED FRUIT DESSERT 🎵

0.35*	114 cals

* plus cooling and chilling time

Serves 8

225 g (8 oz) cherries

225 g (8 oz) blackcurrants or
   redcurrants

450 g (1 lb) strawberries

350 g (12 oz) raspberries

100 g (4 oz) sugar

300 ml ($\frac{1}{2}$ pint) water

thinly pared rind of 2 oranges

60 ml (4 tbsp) orange-flavoured
   liqueur

blanched orange shreds,
   to decorate

1 Prepare the fruit. Stone the cherries, using a cherry pitter if possible to keep them whole.

2 Strig the currants with the prongs of a fork. Hull the strawberries and raspberries.

3 Put the sugar and water in a heavy-based saucepan. Heat gently, stirring occasionally, until the sugar has dissolved. Increase the heat, add the pared orange rind and boil rapidly for 5 minutes, without stirring, to make a sugar syrup.

4 Remove the pan of sugar syrup from the heat and add the cherries and currants. Return to a low heat and simmer gently for 3–5 minutes until only just tender.

5 Add the strawberries and raspberries, fold gently to mix and remove from the heat. Leave until cold.

6 When the fruit and syrup are completely cold, spoon into a glass serving bowl. Discard the orange rind and sprinkle the orange-flavoured liqueur over the fruit. Cover the bowl with cling film and chill in the refrigerator for 2 hours. Sprinkle with the orange shreds before serving.

USEFUL INFORMATION
AND
BASIC RECIPES

Kitchencraft and Cooking Techniques

Busy cooks deserve good tools to work with, and pleasant surroundings in which to work. Often having to conjure up meals in minutes, today's cook can turn to many gadgets and appliances which will make life in the kitchen a lot easier. There is no magic about cooking. There is a simple explanation for everything that happens when a food is cooked. The section on cooking techniques will help you understand why you should cook foods in a certain way in order to prepare them with speed and ease.

KITCHENCRAFT AND COOKING TECHNIQUES

A good cook, like a good craftsman, needs good tools. This does not mean necessarily buying the most expensive equipment and the latest gadgets. It means working out which utensils will be most useful to your style of cooking and eating and making the most of them to save you both time and effort.

The most sophisticated kitchen equipment is of little use if you do not have a well planned kitchen. Kitchens need to have method in the way in which they are laid out; they should save you time and effort in your daily domestic routine; and they should be pleasing places in which to work.

Ingredients for an easy-to-work-in kitchen
Here are some guidelines for use when planning your kitchen. They are aimed at making your time in the kitchen as pleasant and as efficiently spent as possible.
- Make your kitchen physically comfortable, as well as practical to work in.
- Plan activity centres in your kitchen so that they are well positioned in relation to one another.
- These activity centres need, ideally, to be arranged in the logical order for preparing a meal ie store cupboard, preparation area/work surface, and serving/eating area.
- Wherever possible avoid narrow gaps between work surfaces and appliances.
- Store cupboards/larders should allow for the storage of all types of food: dry cupboards for canned and packaged goods; ventilated racks for vegetables and firm fruits. You will also need a refrigerator and a freezer.

- For the work surface choose a durable material, that will withstand fairly hard wear. There should be a good chopping surface, either separate or inset into the work top — wood or some other non-slip surface. Marble and slate are also good as they can serve the dual purpose of chopping surface and a perfect pastry-making surface.
- If possible, keep all large pieces of equipment on the work surface so that they are to hand when you need them. Keep all small preparation equipment and gadgets close to the work surface.
- Storage of saucepans, baking tins etc, depends very much on how your cooking facilities are arranged. If you have a split level cooker, with a hob set into the work surface, then it is advisable to have a cupboard close to the hob; most wall-mounted ovens are set into a housing unit, with drawer space underneath for storing pans and tins.
  With a free-standing cooker, keep all cooking pots and pans, colanders and sieves as close as possible in adjacent cupboards, or hang them on the wall or suspend them from hooks on the ceiling or units.
- Serving and eating areas should, ideally, be close to one another.
- You will also need good lighting, effective ventilation, and a comfortable floor. You need a good source of light directed on all principle work areas. An extractor hood or fan is essential, both to remove excess cooking smells and steam, and to keep the kitchen as cool as possible. The kitchen floor should obviously look nice, but it should also be comfortable to stand on and easy to keep clean. Choose a non-slip surface, which is easy on the feet.

COOKING EQUIPMENT

Choosing the right piece of equipment for a particular job will, in the end, save you time. It pays to invest in good quality equipment as it lasts longer and does the job consistently better than inferior equipment. Here is a guide to the types of equipment you will need to produce delicious food efficiently.

SAUCEPANS

Good pans are usually expensive, but they last; cheap saucepans do not last and often give off toxic metal substances into the food, which is not desirable.

The best pans to use are those made of metals that conduct heat well: copper, cast iron, or good-quality enamelled steel or stainless steel are good choices. Saucepans with a non-stick finish are excellent for boiling milk and making sauces, but they are not such a good choice for some of the 'tougher' cooking jobs. Long term they are a bad buy for the non-stick coating starts to wear off. The heavier the pan the safer it is to use; solid based pans are also less prone to sticking. Handles are another important aspect to be considered when buying pans. If they are riveted they are much more secure than handles which have been screwed on.

Four saucepans of varying sizes, and one good-sized frying pan, is the minimum that you can probably get away with. In addition, most kitchens can make good use of one very large pan, with a handle fixed on either side; it is useful for cooking whole chickens and large pieces of gammon and can double as a preserving pan.

FRYING PANS

Deep frying pans are better than shallow ones; they will hold more food and there is less likelihood of liquids spitting and bubbling over. A lid is essential.

Omelette and pancake pans are by no means musts, but they do make the cooking of both these foods a great deal easier. The sides

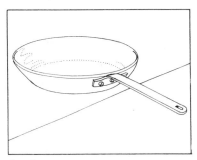

Omelette pan

of an omelette pan are curved and not too high, so that the omelette will roll up readily and fall onto the plate without breaking.

WOKS

A wok is a Chinese cooking utensil which is now very popular in the West as well. It looks like a curve-based large frying pan with two rounded handles and is traditionally made of cast iron though nowadays you can also buy stainless steel and non-stick ones.

Balance it on a metal collar directly over the heat, so that the wok can be moved backwards and forwards to ensure even cooking when stir frying. The wok is a very versatile cooking utensil. Food can be deep fried in it, and then drained on a semi-circular rack which clips on to the rim of the wok; this is very useful when you are frying food in batches. A small circular rack can be positioned in the centre of the wok and used as a steamer with a domed lid fitted neatly over the top.

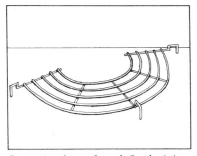

Semi-circular wok rack for draining

FISH KETTLE

A fish kettle is best for poaching whole, large fish. The long oval-shaped pan has handles at either end, and the draining rack that the fish lies on fits neatly inside. The shape of the kettle allows the fish to lie completely flat, without curling; once cooked, the fish can be lifted out easily on the rack, without any danger of it breaking or splitting. If the fish is to be eaten cold it is usually left in the fish kettle in its cooking liquid to cool, and then lifted out.

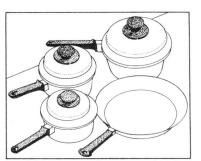

Choose good quality pans

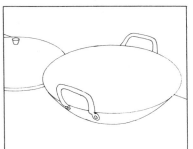

Cast iron wok

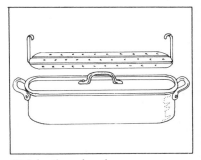

Fish kettle and rack

EGG POACHERS

If you like regular shaped poached eggs, then an egg poacher is the answer. A poacher consists of a base pan (rather like a deep frying pan) which you half fill with water

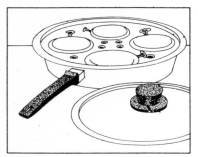

Egg poacher

and a tray containing small poaching cups that sits on top (these are often non-stick). A lid goes over the top of the pan while the eggs are poaching gently in the buttered cups.

BAKING TINS

Baking is a skill; it relies on the precision of the cook, good quality ingredients, and the right shape and size of tin. Even a straight-forward packet cake mix can turn out to be a flop if the wrong tin is used. Most recipes specify a parti-cular size of tin, and this should always be used. Rich mixtures should be baked in strong tins; if the tin is too thin then the mixture will burn.

The greatest worry with baking tins is that of sticking; mixtures that are relatively high in fat are usually fairly safe, but those that contain little fat or are high in sugar, can be very difficult to turn out of a tin.

To line a tin really neatly takes time and patience. The perfect solution is to use baking tins with a non-stick surface; all the familiar shaped tins that are used in every-day baking are available with a non-stick lining. Here is a list of tins you will need for quick, easy baking:

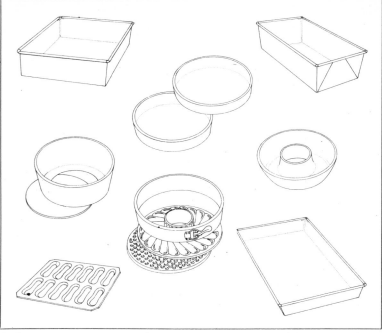

Baking tins: a sandwich tin, loaf tin, round cake tins, madeleine tins and a Swiss roll tin

BASIC TINS

Loaf tins—these come in 450 g (1 lb) and 900 g (2 lb) sizes. Use them for cakes and breadmaking.
Flan rings and tins—use a round tin with plain or fluted sides and a removable base for pastry flans.
Sandwich tins—these come in sizes 18–25.5 cm (7–10 inches) and are shallow, round tins with straight sides for making sandwich and layer cakes. (You can also use spring release tins.)
Swiss roll tins

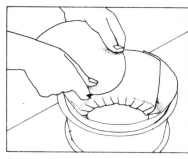

Lining a deep tin for fruit cake

Standard cake tins—you will need 15-cm (6-inch), 16-cm (7-inch) and 17-cm (8-inch) tins.

KNIVES

Good sharp knives are the cook's most important tools. Knives vary enormously in quality, the best ones have taper ground blades—the blade, bolster and tang is forged from one piece of steel, and the handle is fixed securely in place with rivets.
Cook's knives are the classic knives used by all top chefs and professional cooks. They have strong, broad and very sharp blades, and the handles are firmly riveted to give added strength while chopping. Classic cook's knives have heavy handles, there-fore if they fall they land handle first, avoiding damage to the blade. The larger size cook's knives, those with blades between 15–20 cm (6–8 inches) long, are extremely versatile—they can be used for chopping, cubing, slicing, 'mincing', and crushing. Small

Two useful sizes of cook's knife

cook's knives, with blades about 10 cm (4 inches) long are very good for paring vegetables and shaping vegetable garnishes.

Filleting knife

Filleting knives have a long, slim, pliable blade. Sharpness and flexibility are essential, as the blade has to follow the bones of the fish very closely. These knives are also useful for skinning.

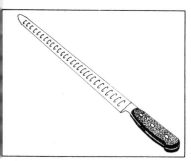

Fishmonger's knife

Fishmonger's knives have a strong, rigid, scalloped blade. These are very heavy knives which make them ideal for cutting through the backbones of fish.

Boning knife

Boning knives have rigid, narrow, broad-backed blades, with very sharp points. They come in different lengths, depending on what they are going to be used to bone. The handles are indented and shaped to prevent your hand from slipping.
Carving knives come in many different styles and sizes. Knives suitable for carving large joints of meat are shaped like an elongated filleting knife; sturdy, but flexible towards the tip of the blade. Serrated knives tend to tear the texture of hot meat, and are best reserved for cutting cold joints.

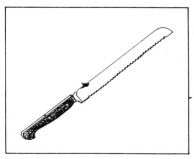

Bread knife with serrated edge

A bread knife should have a fairly rigid blade, but it should be long enough to slice through the largest of loaves—many bread knives have serrated blades, and they tend to cause less crumbs than a plain-edged knife. Serrated knives can also cope with crisp crusts much better.

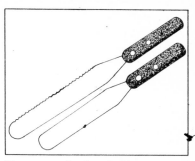

Two types of palette knife

The palette knife gets its name from its artistic associations; it is the same shape as the knife that painters use to mix paint colour with oil. It has a long evenly-wide blade, which is extremely pliable. A palette knife is used primarily for spreading soft mixtures, such as icings, and for flipping foods such as pancakes.

Serrated palette knives are very useful for slicing sponges and other cakes into layers.

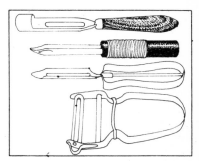

Varieties of potato peeler

Potato peelers are not strictly speaking knives, but they do have a cutting blade and are a must for every kitchen.

CHOPPERS

Choppers have very heavy, deep rectangular blades; they are extremely strong and need to be used with care. They are blade-heavy and tend to drop forward when held. Choppers will cut through most bones, and they are particularly useful for cutting up oxtail. The cleaver is the Chinese equivalent of the chopper, but it is much more versatile; the blade is finer and sharper and can be used for chopping, slicing, 'mincing' and scraping, and for making vegetable garnishes.

SCISSORS

All-purpose kitchen scissors can be used for removing bacon rinds; splitting bread dough decoratively; roughly cutting parsley, chives and other herbs; removing the cores from kidneys.
Fish scissors have serrated blades, with one slightly longer than the other. Use for trimming fins and tails, and cutting through bones.
Poultry shears have a strong spring between the two blades, which makes them extremely robust. They are excellent for cutting through the bones and carcass of all poultry.

KITCHEN SCALES

There are basically two different types of kitchen scales: balance (the traditional variety) and spring balance. Long term, balance scales are a better buy as there is less that can go wrong; unlike spring balance scales they are not dependent on a spring.

Spring balance scales are extremely easy to use and fairly accurate. However, the needle on the dial occasionally gets knocked out of position, so it should be reset each time the scales are used. Some spring balance scales are designed to sit on the work surface, while others can be mounted on the kitchen wall. Unless you have very smooth and level kitchen walls, it is better to buy free-standing scales for accuracy.

Manual juice extractors

SQUEEZERS

Juice squeezers

Juice squeezers or citrus presses come in different shapes and sizes; some are manual and others are operated electrically. The basic principle behind all of them is exactly the same. A ridged dome of glass or plastic presses into the centre of the halved fruit, thus squeezing out the juice. Some of the juicers are hand held, which means that you hold them over a bowl; others have a container beneath the squeezer which collects the juice. Apart from those squeezers which will take halved grapefruits and oranges, there are also smaller ones.

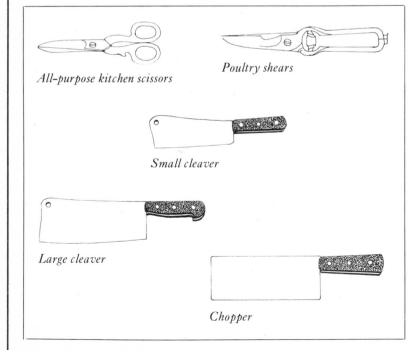

All-purpose kitchen scissors

Poultry shears

Small cleaver

Large cleaver

Chopper

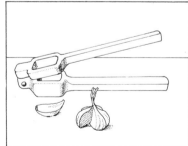

Garlic press

Garlic presses

These are the smallest squeezers of all. They look like small potato ricers, and work in a similar manner. Put the peeled clove of garlic into the press and squeeze down gently—if you squeeze very gently you just get the juice of the garlic—harder, you get the flesh.

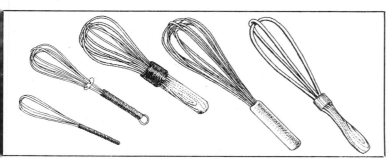

Balloon whisks are available in varying sizes for different tasks

WHISKS

Whisks and beaters cope with a variety of culinary tasks. There are three different kinds of hand whisks: balloon, coiled and rotary. **Balloon whisks** come in different sizes and weights and they are extremely effective. The large, lightweight, very round whisks are the best for egg whites—they are easy to handle and can be used at quite a speed. Slimmer, thicker ridged, and heavier balloon whisks are better for coping with thick sauces, choux pastry or semi-set ice cream mixtures. They will incorporate more air into a mixture than any other type of whisk, and they are extremely easy to clean. **Coiled whisks**, which look just as their name suggests, are cheaper than balloon whisks, but nowhere near as effective. You need to use a lot of effort for not much result. **Rotary whisks** have two four-bladed beaters, which are operated by a small handle. Although you need one hand to steady the whisk and one to turn the handle, it is a speedy and efficient way of whisk-

ing slack mixtures such as egg whites and thin sauces.

Electric whisks and whisk attachments

Hand-operated electric whisks, with two beaters like a rotary whisk, are very efficient. The

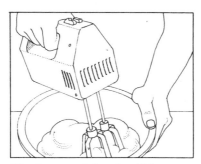

Hand operated electric whisk

beaters can be moved around the inside of a bowl or saucepan (non-stick) with relative ease. This is an advantage when making sauces.

The whisk attachment which goes with several food processors is not that effective; the size of the

beaters is relatively small and they cannot move freely through a mixture to incorporate a noticeable amount of air. It is reasonably effective with whisked cake mixtures, but one must not forget that the bowl of most food processors is relatively small. The whisk attachment on large electric mixers is particularly powerful; it is shaped like a squashed balloon whisk and reaches almost every part of the mixing bowl.

BLENDERS

Electric blenders, also called liquidisers, have become very much an integral part of the kitchen gadget scene. They are extremely labour saving. Some

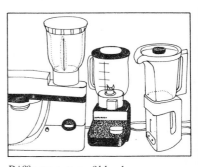

Different types of blender

blenders operate freely as a separate gadget, while others fit onto an electric food mixer. The only way in which they differ tends to be as far as capacity and speed are concerned; some are larger and faster than others. The blades in the base of the plastic or glass goblet rotate at a high speed, pulverising the ingredients inside. It is an invaluable gadget for liquidising soups, sauces, and fruit and vegetable purées, but it can also chop and grind ingredients to varying degrees. There is a hole in the lid of the blender, so ingredients can be dropped through the top while the blades are whirring.

Rotary egg whisk

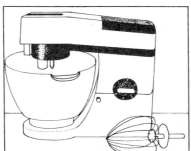

Electric mixer and whisk attachment

ELECTRIC MIXERS AND FOOD PROCESSORS

Electric mixers and food processors can tackle most of the day-to-day culinary tasks, and they are great labour-saving devices for those who are pushed for time and/or have a large family to feed.

The electric mixer

The large size electric mixers, or table mixers as they are often called, have very powerful motors, which can drive a variety of attachments such as: potato peelers, bean shredders and cream makers. The main disadvantage with the table mixer is that it is so bulky, and consequently takes up a lot of space, either on the work surface or in a cupboard. The bowl of the standard table mixer is very capacious, and will hold twice as much as most food processors.

The food processor

The food processor is a compact machine, which is primarily used for chopping, mincing, grinding and blending. It is simple to use, strong, and comparatively quiet. The plastic processor bowl fits over a spindle; the cutting, shredding and whisking attachments in turn fit over the spindle.

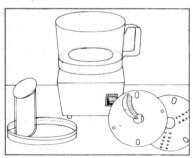

Food processor showing blades

The lid that fits over the bowl has a funnel through which food or liquid can be fed. When the machine is turned on, the cutting blade or other attachments move very fast—vegetables are chopped in 10 seconds, minced in

15 seconds, and puréed in 20 seconds. Food processors have revolutionsed some of our methods of preparation, for example, they are a great help when making pastry and bread doughs, soups, pâtés and terrines.

A word of warning: even though you can buy whisking attachments for food processors, they are not as effective as the beaters on a traditional electric table mixer.

MINCERS

This useful gadget quickly turns cooked or raw meat, fish and vegetables into tiny particles. It is an asset when using up leftover cooked food and is also excellent for preparing your own freshly minced meat at home.

Hand mincers are usually made from cast iron or a strong plastic. They fit firmly onto the work surface, either by means of small rubber suction pads or a screw clamp; the latter is the most secure, and the larger mincers are always fitted with a clamp. The handle on the mincer turns a 'screw' which pushes the food to be minced towards small cutting blades or extruding discs. The size of the perforations in the metal discs dictates the final texture of the minced food, which will either be fine, medium or coarse.

Mincer attachments can also be bought to fit into many table electric mixers.

PRESSURE COOKERS

Pressure cookers can save you a great deal of time. There are many different models available, but basically a pressure cooker looks like a heavy duty saucepan, with a domed lid. It has a weight on it which helps determine the level of pressure at which the food will cook and it also has a safety valve for steam to escape. It works on the principle of increasing the boiling temperature of water and then trapping the resultant steam. (This is achieved by means of added pressure.) Some models of

pressure cooker only operate under one pressure; however, the more recent models operate under three; so you can choose which pressure to use according to the type of food you are cooking.

The food is put into the base of the cooker with the appropriate amount of liquid; the lid is then firmly closed and the pan placed over the heat until steam comes through the vents. The necessary pressure weight is then added until a hissing noise is emitted; at this point the heat is turned down for the remainder of the cooking time. (This is always indicated in individual recipes.) After cooking, the pressure has to be released, either slowly or quickly, depending on the food inside. Most recent pressure cookers have an automatic setting on the lid, complete with a timer; this enables you to set both the cooking time and the speed at which pressure should be released.

The pressure cooker is particularly good for cooking the following types of foods:

STOCKS AND SOUPS

Meat—the less expensive, tougher cuts
Poultry and game (especially boiling fowl and casserole game)
Firm textured fish (pressure cooking eliminates the fishy smell)
Root vegetables, such as swedes
Pulses
Grain—brown rice
Steamed puddings—both sweet and savoury

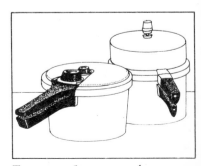

Two types of pressure cooker

Preserves—jams, marmalade, bottled fruits and chutney

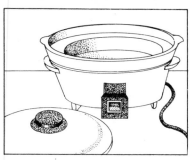

Crockpot or slow cooker

CROCKPOTS

Cooking in a crockpot (or slow-cooker) is an up-dated version of a traditional method of cooking: our great-grandmothers would leave casseroles cooking gently all day in the very coolest part of the kitchen range.

The crockpot consists of an earthenware bowl which sits neatly inside an outer casing. An electric element is fixed between the base of the bowl and the casing, and it operates on two settings—low (75 watts) and high (130 watts). When plugged in it only uses about the same amount of power as a light bulb.

As the name suggests, a crock-pot or slow-cooker cooks foods very slowly; so slowly that it can cook food while you are out of the house. It saves time, money and fuel. With most recipes, all the ingredients can be put into the crockpot at once and then left to cook for several hours. The steam which condenses on the crockpot lid returns to the pot, thus keeping the food moist. Subtle, rich flavours develop during long, slow cooking, and it is ideal for the tougher and cheaper cuts of meat. The crockpot heats very gently so there is no risk of burning, sticking or boiling over; consequently it is very easy to clean. Food does not need to be stirred during cooking and it is important to resist the temptation to remove the lid while cooking. If it is removed,

heat is lost from the crockpot and it takes a long time for the original temperature to be regained.

General guidelines
- The crockpot needs pre-heating before food is added.
- Meat has a better appearance and flavour if it is lightly fried before it goes into the crockpot.
- Always bring stock and other liquids to the boil before adding them to the crockpot.
- Most foods should be started off on the High setting, and then reduced to Slow for the remainder of the time; chicken and pork to be 'roasted' should be cooked on High for the whole cooking time.
- Always follow the given quantities of liquid in a recipe accurately; too much liquid can result in overcooking.
- Meats with a high fat content should be trimmed very well before being put into the crockpot; fats do not bake-off as they do in a conventional oven.
- A crockpot should not be used for re-heating any cooked frozen food.
- Leftovers from food that has been cooked in a crockpot must be brought to boiling point in a saucepan before being eaten.

A crockpot is suitable for cooking most foods, as long as recipes are adapted accordingly. It is, however, particularly successful when preparing the following:

Soups
Cooked pâtés
Root vegetables
Meat and poultry—casseroles and 'roasts'
Fish casseroles
Cheese fondue
Steamed puddings
Rice pudding (and other grain puddings)
Lemon curd

COOKING BRICKS
Cooking bricks are simplicity itself to use and always produce delicious-tasting, moist and tender

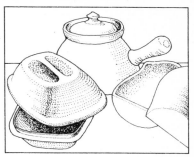

Unglazed, earthenware cooking bricks

food. They come in a variety of shapes and sizes and can be used for cooking most meats, fish and even potatoes, although they always tend to be referred to as 'chicken bricks'. Made of porous, unglazed earthenware, with close-fitting lids, these bricks are very similar in concept to the clay pots used in Greek and Roman times. Before using a brick, always give it a preliminary soaking in cold water each time that you use it in order for it to impart moisture to the food being cooked.

After draining, place the seasoned food into the cooking brick with herbs, chopped vegetables, and any other flavourings or seasonings that you like, and put the lid on top. Put the brick into a cold oven, and then turn it on. As the oven heats up, condensation forms on the lid of the brick, and trickles back onto the food; this acts as a baste and keeps the food moist. All the flavour, juices and aroma of the food are conserved naturally, and the food is far less fatty than it is when cooked by many other more conventional methods, such as roasting or frying.

Cooking bricks should never be washed with detergent as this will taint the food. Just wipe out well with a clean damp cloth or wash in water to which a little vinegar has been added. The bricks do darken with use, but this does not mean that they are dirty, just discoloured.

ELECTRIC DEEP FRYERS

Many people avoid deep frying if they can, because they hate the smell and mess that are associated with it. However careful you are when deep frying food in an open fryer, you cannot prevent the lingering odour. Frying in hot deep fat can also be extremely dangerous. If the temperature of the fat is not regulated very carefully, it can burn; and if moisture gets into the hot fat, it can bubble up and boil over. Electrically operated deep fryers are not only safer, but they also guarantee successful results every time and there is little or no smell. Most electric deep fryers are thermostatically controlled, so that the temperature of the fat or oil is controlled automatically. When the fryer is plugged in and switched on, an indicator light comes on; once the desired temperature of the oil or fat has been reached, the light goes out. The

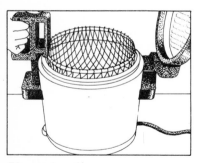

Electric deep fryer

frying basket clips onto the inside of the fryer and can be fixed at various heights. This enables you to put the food that is to be fried into the basket, before the oil or fat is heated—there is no need to lift the lid of the fryer off, as the basket can be lowered into the hot fat from the outside of the fryer. A special filter is fitted into the lid of the fryer which neutralises all the fat and cooking smells. The controlled temperature of the fat ensures that foods are fried to just the right degree.

COOKING TECHNIQUES

When cooking you can use a variety of different techniques from grilling to frying and roasting to poaching. As well as understanding all the techniques you must also bear in mind the type of food that you are going to cook and the time you have to cook it in. Under each technique are given guidelines as to which foods are best suited to this particular method of preparation.

Here are some quick and easy techniques—including grilling and frying—as well as a number of longer cooking methods, like casseroling. Once you have grasped the basics of these you will find them extraordinarily straightforward.

QUICK AND EASY COOKING METHODS
GRILLING

Grilling is one of the simplest and quickest methods of cooking. It simply involves placing the food under the heat source, turning it and then removing it when cooked. Generally, small pieces of food are grilled like chicken portions, sausages or fish fillets, all of which cook relatively quickly.

To perfect the technique always preheat the grill before using it. The high temperature sears the surface of the food, sealing in all the juices, before cooking continues. With thick pieces of food, such as steaks or chops, sear both sides, but you do not need to do this with finer foods such as thin cutlets or fillets of fish, ideal foods when you are in a hurry. To speed up cooking time place foods to be seared near the source of heat, then lower the grill pan for the remainder of the cooking time.

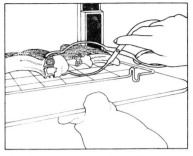

Turning meat under the grill

To make the food taste its best keep it moist throughout grilling; brush it from time to time with oil, melted butter or a marinade. However, do not be tempted to season meat with salt until after it has been cooked as this can toughen it. Test the food while it is cooking to see if it is done.

When grilling chicken and pork, always grill them very thoroughly to ensure that they are cooked through. Steak and lamb, however, can be cooked according to personal preference and to the amount of time available.

Use tongs for turning the food during grilling, and never pierce it with a fork or skewer or you may get hot fat sprayed at you. Always serve grilled foods immediately as they dry out quickly and toughen if kept warm.

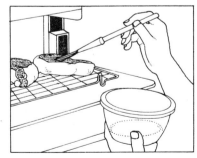

Brushing meat with marinade

IDEAL GRILLING FOODS

Beef—steaks (fillet, rump, sirloin, entrecôte and T-bone), sausages and beefburgers

Lamb—chump chops, loin chops, cutlets, leg steaks (cut from fillet end), liver and kidneys

Pork—fillet, spare-rib chops, loin chops, sausages, liver and kidney

Bacon and Gammon—rashers and chops

Veal—fillet (as kebabs), cutlets, loin chops, liver (calf's)

Chicken—breasts, drumsticks, leg and wing joints, split and flattened poussins

Fish—thick fillets, steaks, small whole fish

Mushrooms

Tomatoes

FRYING

Foods can be deep fried, shallow fried or stir fried. It is useful to have all these ways of cooking at your fingertips since they all give quick results and are easy to do once you have mastered the technique. Basically they all depend on two simple principles which are that you use relatively small pieces of food and that you use hot fat to cook them in.

DEEP FRYING

A variety of foods can be successfully deep fried from potatoes to cheese, chicken and fish. Indeed, entire meals can be deep fried.

The technique involves heating a large amount of oil, usually vegetable oil, in a solid-based pan or deep-fat fryer, lowering food into it, letting it cook for a few minutes and then taking it out. Here are some steps on deep frying.

Steps to deep frying

Fill a heavy-based pan no more than two-thirds full of oil. Start heating the oil very gently at first, and then raise the heat. Check the temperature of the oil carefully, either by using a frying thermometer, or test with a cube of stale bread (see below).

- Coat the foods for deep frying

with breadcrumbs or batter, this protects them while being cooked and also prevents

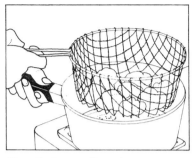

Deep frying small portions

moisture from the food leaking into the oil.

- When cooking small portions or pieces of food, lower them into the fat in a wire frying basket; this makes it easier to remove them from the hot fat.
- Always lower the food into the hot oil slowly.
- Once the food is cooked, remove it carefully using a wire basket or a perforated spoon, and drain on absorbent kitchen paper.
- Remove all crumbs and remnants of fried food with a perforated spoon, otherwise they will burn and taint the flavour of the oil. Do not allow water or other liquids to get into the fat or it will 'spit'.
- Turn the heat off as soon as

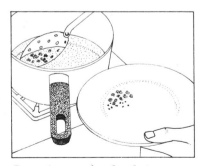

Removing crumbs after frying

you have finished deep frying, and leave the pan to cool without moving it.

Straining cooled oil for storage

- Once the oil is quite cool, strain it thoroughly, and store in a clean bottle for future use.

Deep frying temperatures

The temperature of hot oil for deep frying varies considerably according to the type of food and on whether it is raw or has already been cooked. Raw food is cooked at a lower temperature than cooked. A frying thermometer is the most accurate method of gauging the heat of the oil; alternatively, use a cube of day-old bread.

The bread cube method

- If the bread cube sinks to the bottom of the pan of oil, and does not frizzle at all, then the oil is not yet hot enough.
- If the bread cube frizzles gently, then the oil has reached about 180°C (350°F) and you can fry beignets and do the 'first frying' of chipped potatoes.
- If a light blue haze rises from the oil and the bread cube browns in 1 minute then the oil has reached about 190°C (375°F) and is at the right temperature for frying coated fish fillets, croquettes and fruit fritters.
- If a noticeable blue haze rises from the oil and the bread cube browns in 30 seconds, then the oil has reached about 200°C (400°F) and it is ready for frying small fritters, croûtons, coated cooked foods (such as fish cakes), and the second frying of chipped potatoes.

SHALLOW FRYING

Shallow frying is another quick and easy method of cooking, although not quite as quick as deep frying. It is ideal for cooking chops, steaks, escalopes, liver, sausages, bacon, eggs and fish. All you need to do is fry the food in a shallow amount of hot fat (about 1–2.5 cm/½–1 inch) over a moderate heat. Turn the food once during cooking. You can use a variety of fats from cooking oil, vegetable oil, olive oil, white cooking fat, lard, margarine, butter, or a mixture. If you want to use butter don't use it on its own as it burns at a relatively low temperature. It is advisable to mix it with oil or margarine.

It is best to coat the food before shallow frying it; this helps to protect it from the temperature of the fat, and also prevents fragile items, such as fish fillets, from collapsing.

The guidelines for safe and successful shallow frying are very similar to those for deep fat frying, although there are distinct differences. The fat must be heated gently at all times, even during the actual cooking; there is no need to use a fat thermometer to test the heat of the oil, just drop a small piece of stale bread into the hot fat and it should sizzle steadily without spitting. Lower the coated food into the hot fat gently, and turn it during frying with a per-

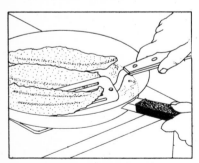

Turning food during frying

forated spoon or fish slice. (Scoop off any crumbs or remnants of food from the surface of the cooking fat so they don't burn.)

Remove the cooked food with a perforated spoon or slice and drain thoroughly.

STIR FRYING

Stir frying is a traditional Chinese method of cooking, which has gained tremendous popularity throughout Europe in recent years. It is a quick and versatile technique that can be used for vegetables, meat, fish, rice and noodles. The secret of the technique lies in cutting up the food into uniformly-sized small pieces and then cooking them very quickly in oil. The beauty of this method of cooking is that the food retains its shape, texture and taste.

A wok, the traditional Chinese cooking utensil, is the best receptacle to use for stir frying. It is a large, deep metal pan, with a completely spherical base and two looped handles.

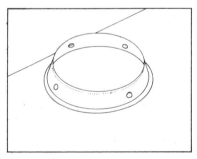

Metal collar to support wok on ring

Place the wok directly on the gas or electric ring. (It works better on gas.) You can buy a metal collar which you fit around your cooking ring, which acts as a support for the wok. This makes it easier to move the wok around as the food is cooking, ensuring that each surface of the wok comes in contact with an even temperature; an all essential fact in stir frying.

When you stir fry foods you'll find that they cook very quickly, so it's important to have everything well prepared in advance. Chop your food up into evenly-sized small pieces and, if using meat or fish, coat it in flour. Place

the wok over the heat, preferably standing on a metal collar, and add a few spoonfuls of oil to it. Once the oil is hot, add the finely cut ingredients, either all in one go or in stages, depending on the recipe. Garlic, root ginger and other highly flavoured ingredients are often used. These should be fried first and then the other ingredients should be added. Tilt the wok backwards and forwards

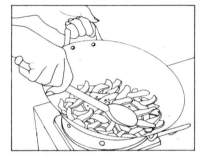

Tilting wok while stir-frying

over the heat, while you stir and turn the ingredients with a long-handled spatula until cooked.

POACHING

This is a subtle cooking technique used for preparing delicate foods which cook quickly. Poaching describes the gentle agitation of a hot liquid by natural movement of the liquid. Odd bubbles occur, but not the steady bubbling that one associates with simmering. The choice of cooking liquid depends

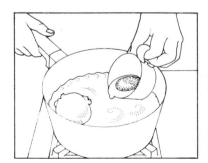

Poaching eggs in hot liquid

to a large extent on what you are poaching; for fish, a court bouillon or wine would be most appropriate; for meat, a vegetable or meat stock or wine; for eggs, water.

When poaching eggs and quenelles, add them to the liquid, once it is hot and 'quivering'. Fish fillets, on the other hand, should be put into the pan with cold liquid and then brought to the correct temperature for poaching. Fish is usually poached covered, but many other foods are poached without a lid.

Suitable poaching foods
Boned and skinned chicken breasts
Meat and fish quenelles
Fish fillets and thin fish cutlets
Shellfish, such as scallops
Eggs
Gnocchi
Soft fruits, such as peaches

STEAMING
This is a quick and nutritious way of cooking food and is generally applied to vegetables. All you need is a simple metal steamer which you place in a saucepan. Pour in

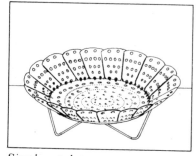

Simple metal steamer

boiling water to just beneath the steamer, add the vegetables and cover with a lid. The vegetables will cook in the steam and, unlike when they are cooked in water, very little nutritious value will be lost. Steaming is also an excellent way of reheating food.

SLOW BUT EASY
There are a number of cooking techniques that fall under this heading: roasting, barbecuing, pot roasting, casseroling, boiling, poaching and steaming. They are

all easy and once the cooking is underway require little supervision.

ROASTING
Roasting is certainly a very effortless way of cooking. Once the food is in the oven, you can virtually forget about it, apart from giving it the occasional baste. However, roasting is only suitable for prime, tender cuts of meat, and for poultry and most game.

Roasting is a direct heat method of cooking, and the food needs to be kept moist throughout cooking. Before putting the joint or bird into the oven spread it with fat (duck is the only exception to this rule—it is naturally fatty and should be pricked with a skewer before roasting). With meat, poultry or game that dries out quickly, like chicken, veal, venison, pheasant and grouse, it is advisable to cover it with strips of

Adding moisture with strips of bacon

streaky bacon. This gives added moisture.

Veal, lamb and pork can be boned, stuffed and rolled before roasting as can poultry and game. Use a well-flavoured stuffing which will moisten and enhance the flavour of the meat during cooking. Stuffing makes the meat go further, but it takes longer to cook.

Another way of keeping the food moist during roasting, is to cover it with cooking foil, dull side uppermost; the foil can be removed either for the first or last part of the cooking time, to allow the food to brown. When using

foil, add on an extra few minutes cooking time.

Place your meat, poultry or feathered game on a grid or rack in a roasting tin. This is important since it makes it easy to baste the food during cooking and to roast vegetables under it.

Roast in a preheated oven for the given time, basting with the

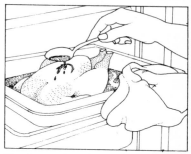

Basting poultry during cooking

juices and fat in the roasting tin from time to time. Test to see whether the meat is done. Push a skewer right into the meat, take it out and feeling it, when it is hot to the touch the meat is done. Beef, lamb and game are often served underdone, but chicken, turkey and pork should always be cooked right through. If you are using a meat thermometer, insert the thermometer in the thickest part of the meat before it goes into the oven, making sure that it does not touch the bone. All roast meats are

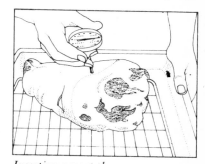

Inserting a meat thermometer

much easier to carve or cut if they are first allowed to 'settle' after cooking. Remove from the oven and keep warm for about 15 minutes until ready to serve.

What to roast
Beef—whole fillet, rump, fore rib, sirloin on the bone, boned sirloin, wing rib, topside, silverside
Lamb—leg, best end of neck, breast, shoulder, loin
Pork—whole fillet, spare rib, hand and spring, belly, loin, blade
Veal—loin, leg, shoulder, breast, best end of neck
Poultry—chicken, poussins, turkey, duck, guinea fowl
Game (young)—wild duck, pheasant, pigeon, grouse, venison.

Roasting times and methods
There are three basic methods of roasting (see chart for methods and timing).

Method A
The meat is first roasted at 230°C (450°F) mark 8, for 15 minutes, and the heat is then reduced to 180°C (350°F) mark 4, for the remainder of the cooking time.

Method B
The meat is roasted at 190°C (375°F) mark 5 for the whole cooking time.

Method C
The meat is roasted at 160°C (325°F) mark 3 for the whole cooking time. This long slow method of roasting is most suitable for large turkeys, and for joints which are not considered prime roasting joints like, for example, silverside of beef, hand and spring of pork and breast of lamb.

Remember to allow extra roasting time if foil and/or stuffing are used, and to weigh joints and birds *after* stuffing in order to calculate accurate cooking time.

	Methods A & B	Method C
Beef (whole fillet, rump, sirloin, ribs, topside, silverside)	15–20 minutes for every 450 g (1 lb) plus 20 minutes	30 minutes for every 450 g (1 lb) plus 30 minutes
Lamb (leg shoulder, loin, best end of neck, breast)	20–25 minutes for every 450 g (1 lb) plus 25 minutes	35–40 minutes for every 450 g (1 lb) plus 40 minutes
Pork (whole fillet, loin, leg, sparerib, hand and spring, belly, loin, blade)	30 minutes for every 450 g (1 lb) plus 30 minutes	40–45 minutes for every 450 g (1 lb) plus 45 minutes
Veal (loin, leg, shoulder, breast, best end of neck)	25–30 minutes for every 450 g (1 lb) plus 30 minutes	35–40 minutes for every 450 g (1 lb) plus 40 minutes
Chicken (whole bird)	20 minutes for every 450 g (1 lb) plus 20 minutes	30 minutes for every 450 g (1 lb) plus 30 minutes
Turkey 2.25–3.5 kg (5–8 lb)	20 minutes for every 450 g (1 lb) plus 20 minutes	30 minutes for every 450 g (1 lb) plus 30 minutes
3.5–6.5 kg (8–14 lb)	—	20 minutes for every 450 g (1 lb) plus 20 minutes
Over 6.5 kg (14 lb)	—	15 minutes for every 450 g (1 lb) plus 15 minutes
Duck	15 minutes for every 450 g (1 lb) plus 15 minutes	20 minutes for every 450 g (1 lb) plus 20 minutes

BARBECUING
Barbecuing is a wonderfully easy way of cooking food out of doors. It lends itself perfectly to entertaining, since you can get delicious results with the minimum of effort.

A barbecue is like an outdoor grill, depending on charcoal for its fuel. The grill needs to be heated first and then the meat or fish which is to be cooked is placed either directly on the grill or first in foil and then on the grill.

Preparing food for barbecuing
- Always use good-quality meat; poor quality meat does not cook very well on a barbecue
- Marinate the food for at least 1 hour before barbecuing it. This enhances its flavour and ensures moistness
- Allow chilled foods to come to room temperature before putting them on the barbecue; chilled foods give off moisture which can cause spitting
- Brush foods with oil to prevent them from sticking to the barbecue grill
- Season meat and poultry with salt after cooking as salt draws off the meat juices
- Watch food carefully once it is on the barbecue, and test from time to time.
- As well as barbecuing directly on the barbecue grill, food can also be wrapped in foil and cooked either on the grill or in the coals

Good foods for barbecues
Beef—lean steaks, good stewing (kebabs)
Lamb—chops, leg steaks, fillet (kebabs)
Pork—chops, spare-ribs, fillet (kebabs)
Bacon and sausages
Veal—chops, leg fillet (kebabs)
Chicken—drumsticks, legs, split poussins
Offal—kidneys
Fish—firm-textured fish such as halibut, monkfish and cod; whole fish such as bass, bream, trout,

mackerel and sardines
Shellfish—split lobster, large prawns and scallops
Vegetables—corn on the cob is particularly good
Fruit—particularly bananas, cubes or slices threaded on skewers, in their skins or skinned and wrapped in foil

POT ROASTING

This is a one-pot method of cooking larger pieces of meat, whole birds and fish. It involves the minimum of preparation and long, slow cooking. Simply brown the meat all over in hot fat in a heavy pan, remove from the pan while browning vegetables in the fat. Place the meat on top of the vegetables; add a little liquid, cover and cook in a moderate oven.

For an even quicker pot roast use the cold start method and simply put all the ingredients in the pot at once and place in the oven. The cooking time will be longer.

Good foods to pot roast
Brisket or topside of beef; boned, stuffed and rolled breast of lamb or veal; stuffed hearts; rolled shoulder of venison and chicken.

CASSEROLING

With very little preparation and long, slow cooking you have a dish that can be prepared in advance and then reheated as required. Casseroles freeze very well and can be brought to the table in their casserole dish. In short, they save you a great deal of time.

There are two types of casseroles—brown (fry start) and white (cold start). To make a brown casserole, fry small chunks of meat in fat until browned all over. Remove and drain on absorbent kitchen paper. Add vegetables to the pan and fry until well coated. Add seasoning, stir in some flour, put back the meat and add some liquid. Cover tightly and simmer either on top of the cooker or in a slow to medium oven until tender. A white casserole is

quicker to prepare. Simply layer the same ingredients as for a brown casserole into your dish and place in a slow to moderate oven, cooking until tender.

GOOD FOODS FOR CASSEROLING

Beef—leg, shin, chuck, flank, blade, skirt, joints of topside, top rump, brisket, silverside
Lamb—breast, scrag, middle or best end of neck, loin. Shoulder and leg may be cooked as joints or boned and cubed
Pork—hand, spare rib, belly (trimmed of fat). Also, loin chops, spare rib chops and fillet. Gammon steaks and joints and cooked, cubed ham
Veal—breast, neck, shoulder, shin, leg, knuckle
Offal—ox and sheep's kidneys; calves' and sheep hearts; lambs' and sheep's tongues; oxtail
Poultry—joints
Game—grouse, rabbit
Pulses

BOILING

Boiling is an easy technique that involves covering the food in a liquid, heating it until it comes to boiling point and then, more often than not, lowering the heat and simmering it. The cooking time will depend on what type of food is being cooked as well as its size. You can boil meat, fish, grains, pulses and vegetables.

Boiling meat and poultry
Tie or truss joints and poultry carefully with string, so that they retain their shape during cooking. Smoked and salty gammon and ham should be soaked in cold water before hand and the soaking water should be discarded. This gets rid of some of the saltiness. Place the meat or poultry in a large pan with enough cold water to cover. Bring to the boil. Lower the heat and remove any surface scum with a slotted spoon. Add chopped onion, some chopped peeled root vegetables, a bay leaf, a small bunch of parsley, a few

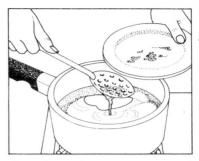
Removing surface scum

peppercorns and a blade of mace. (Add salt at the end of the cooking time or the meat will toughen. Don't add it to pickled or cured meat.) Cover the pan tightly and simmer very gently. The exact time depends on the type of meat; with boiling fowl it depends on age. As an approximate guide, allow 30 minutes for every 450 g (1 lb), plus an extra 30 minutes.

Suitable meats for boiling
Beef—brisket or silverside
Lamb—leg of mutton
Pork—belly
Gammon and bacon—corner gammon, middle gammon, gammon slipper, boned and rolled hock
Poultry—boiling fowl
Grains
Pulses
Vegetables

Freezing and Other Handy Tricks

Owning a freezer is rather like having a second pair of hands in the kitchen. You need a pastry case: don't bake one, take it out of the freezer! You want some real stock for special dish; don't make some, thaw some! If you have a culinary disaster—never mind—here's how to turn it into a success. Plus some tricks of the trade to make the simplest dishes look and taste superb.

FREEZING

Careful and thoughtful use of your freezer not only speeds up your cooking, but it makes it a lot easier. Never be tempted to freeze food for the sake of filling the freezer; you should only freeze food that you and your family like and that you will enjoy serving to guests.

Your freezer should be a great help when it comes to planning menus, especially for parties and other large functions. Food from your freezer should always be complemented by seasonal fresh foods, both to give you satisfaction as the cook, and to offer variety. No one is going to be particularly impressed by eating frozen raspberries when fresh ones are in season. Watch this overlap carefully when planning menus.

Apart from freezing made-up dishes, freezers are immensely useful for storing odd bits and pieces which will speed up food preparation. Things like, for example, breadcrumbs, grated cheese, chopped fresh herbs and leftover wine. All these can be added to the freezer in a spare moment and are indispensable when cooking in a hurry.

Do not be tempted to put food in your freezer and forget about it. Always label foods clearly. Although food that is kept past its recommended storage time is perfectly edible and safe to eat, it will deteriorate somewhat in flavour, texture and appearance.

Always use very fresh ingredients; the food that you take out of the freezer is only as good as the food that you put in. Freeze foods in amounts that you know you will use in one go; it is usually impossible to separate out small quantities from a larger pack. People tend to disagree on which foods can be frozen and which cannot. In fact all foods *can* be frozen, but the thawed result is often far from acceptable. It is the water content in food which freezes first; if the water content of a food is very high, the food will collapse on thawing. Two very good examples are raw lettuce and cucumber; it would be an absolute disaster to try and freeze either. However, they can be frozen in the form of soup.

WHAT TO FREEZE

SOUPS

It is a very practical proposition to freeze soups. Always make them in large quantities as they freeze particularly well. Soups based on vegetable purées freeze best of all. Homemade stocks give a better flavour to soup that is to be frozen; any excess stock can always be frozen separately. Cool soup very quickly after making it, pack it in suitable sized containers, and freeze it as soon as possible. If a soup needs cream, it is advisable to add it on reheating, otherwise it may separate.

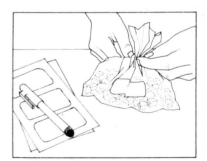

Packing croûtons for freezing

Croûtons are handy soup garnishes and can be frozen, already fried, in freezer bags. They can be 'freshened up' from frozen in a moderately hot oven.

GOOD SOUPS FOR FREEZING

Carrot and orange soup; cauliflower soup; French onion soup and potato and watercress soup.

Recommended storage life: 3 months.

FISH

Fish is a highly perishable food, and even more care has to be taken when you are buying it for the freezer, than when buying it to be eaten fresh. Make a good friend of your fishmonger, so that you can rely on him choosing really good quality fish for you. Always freeze fish the day it is bought. If you are freezing uncooked fresh fish pack it in such a way that you will be able to take out just the quantity that you need; interleave fillets

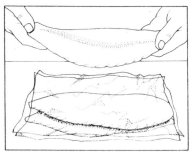

Interleaving fillets with freezer wrap

and steaks with freezer wrap. White fish stands up to freezing far better than shellfish and smoked fish.

GOOD FISH DISHES FOR FREEZING

Cod provençale; fish loaf; home-made fish cakes; smoked fish mousses; smoked haddock croquettes and salmon quiche.

Recommended storage life: 2 months for dishes containing white fish; 1 month for dishes using smoked or shellfish.

CHEESE

Cheese does not freeze very well in its raw state as it tends to lose texture and become crumbly. Bags of grated cheese are useful to have in the freezer—frozen grated cheese is free-flowing and useful when in a hurry. Made up dishes containing cheese freeze most successfully. Some cheese dishes are best frozen uncooked or only partly cooked.

GOOD CHEESE DISHES FOR FREEZING

Croquettes; cheese and ham flan and pizza.

Recommended storage life: 2 months.

MEAT AND POULTRY

Most varieties of meat and poultry freeze extremely well, both raw and made up into complete dishes. Dishes that take time and effort to prepare are the ones to freeze. They are invariably the sort of dishes that are perfect for un-expected dinner guests or for family meals. Pasta-based dishes; cooked meat or poultry in a gravy or sauce; homemade beefburgers or meatballs are all excellent from the freezer. When making cas-seroles for the freezer, reduce the initial cooking time by about 30 minutes. Casseroles are best thawed before reheating; it is safer, and the texture of the ingredients is much better.

GOOD MEAT AND POULTRY DISHES FOR FREEZING

Meat and chicken casseroles; chicken Kiev; meat loaves; pâtés and terrines; meat fillings (to use for pies); pasta dishes such as lasagne; mince based dishes such as moussaka; beefburgers and meatballs; beef olives.

Recommended storage life: 3 months.

TO FREEZE A CASSEROLE

Line a casserole dish with freezer foil and fill with the cooled, cooked casserole. Pinch the foil over to seal, and freeze until solid. Lift out the foil parcel with the frozen casserole in it, and over-wrap. Return to the freezer. (In this way you are not minus a cas-serole dish.) When you want to use the frozen casserole: take it out of the freezer, remove the wrap-ping and place the solid casserole back into the casserole dish in which it was originally cooked Allow it to thaw and then reheat. No messy freezer containers, and the casserole looks as if it has been cooked in the dish in which you serve it.

SAUCES AND STOCKS

Sweet and savoury sauces are both very worthwhile items to have in the freezer; they save a lot of time and last-minute effort. Choose sauces that are versatile. Basic white or brown sauces are both good; they are useful in their own right but can also be used as the base for many other simple sauces. Thickened sauces stand up to freezing far better if they are thickened with cornflour rather than with wheat flour. For sweet sauces, freeze those based on a fruit purée or pulp, and smooth sauces like those made from chocolate. Sauces are best frozen in quite small quantities (even in ice cube trays); amounts that you can use in one go. The most con-venient way of packing sauces which are to be served hot, is to use 'boil-in-the-bag' bags; they can quickly be thawed and heated be lowering them into a pan of boiling water.

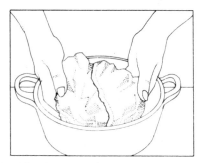

Lifting out parcel of frozen casserole

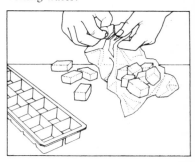

Packing frozen stock cubes

GOOD SAUCES FOR FREEZING

Basic brown sauce; basic white sauce; Bolognese sauce; curry sauce; fresh tomato sauce and onion sauce.

Apple; butterscotch; chocolate and cranberry.

Recommended storage life: 6 months for most, but 2 months for those containing strong flavours such as curry, or perishable ingredients such as meat.

DESSERTS AND PUDDINGS

The perfect puddings to have in your freezer are those which can be taken out and are ready to serve as soon as they have thawed. Dessert 'bases' are also very useful to have on hand in the freezer, such as, pastry cases, sponge cases and choux buns.

Homemade ice creams are easy to prepare when you have a freezer, and are far superior to the bought varieties. Cooked fruit purées are very useful; once thawed they can be topped with pastry lids or crumble mixtures. Pies can be baked before freezing, or left uncooked, in which case they can be cooked from frozen; if you use foil pie plates, make sure that the fruit does not come in contact with the foil as the fruit acid reacts on foil.

GOOD DESSERTS AND PUDDINGS FOR FREEZING

Flans; flan cases; fruit pies and purées; ice creams, homemade and profiteroles (freeze choux buns and chocolate sauce separately); mousses and soufflés.

Recommended storage life: up to 6 months for most puddings and desserts.

DESSERT AND PUDDING GARNISHES

CRUNCHY BISCUIT CRUMBS

Crumble stale biscuits into crumbs; fry in butter with a little demerara sugar. Cool and freeze in a freezer bag. Use frozen to crumble over ice creams or as a cheat crumble topping.

LEMON SLICES

Open freeze thin slices, or half slices, of lemon. Pack into freezer bags. Once thawed they can be used for decorating puddings and desserts, or for adding to drinks.

WHIPPED CREAM ROSETTES

Pipe rosettes of whipped cream

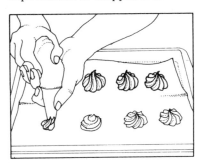

Piping rosettes of whipped cream

onto waxed paper and open freeze. Pack into rigid containers, separating layers and return to the freezer. Thaw on absorbent kitchen paper, before placing on top of the pudding or dessert.

BAKING

Nearly all baked foods, such as cakes, breads and biscuits, freeze extremely well. Many of them are also quite time-consuming to make, so it is a great advantage to be able to freeze them. Baked foods also tend to go stale quite quickly; the freezer keeps them beautifully fresh until required. All baked goods should be really cold before they are packed for the freezer. Thin icings can go very runny on thawing so it is better to

stick to the thicker types such as buttercreams and frostings. Cakes or gâteaux which have a piped or elaborate decoration on top should always be 'open-frozen' before being packed.

GOOD BAKED ITEMS FOR FREEZING

Brandy snaps; bread, all types; cheesecakes; chocolate cake; éclairs (unfilled); scones (sweet or savoury); sponge cake layers (ready for assembly).

Recommended storage time: about 2 months.

Breadcrumbs: When you have some slightly stale bread, make it into breadcrumbs, and freeze in freezer bags. (They are very useful in savoury cooking as well as in sweet recipes.

VEGETABLES AND FRUIT

If there is a glut of any particular fruit, or you happen to have it growing in the garden, then it is always worth freezing some down for using later in the year. Raspberries and blackberries are both good choices.

The same really applies to vegetables, as far as freezing them in their natural state is concerned. Some made up vegetable dishes also freeze very well; two good examples are stuffed peppers and stuffed aubergines.

GOOD VEGETABLES AND FRUITS FOR FREEZING

Asparagus, broad beans, broccoli, Brussels sprouts, calabrese, carrots, cauliflower, courgettes, fennel, leeks, mangetout, peas, peppers, runner beans and sweetcorn.

Apples, blackberries, blackcurrants, damsons, gooseberries, greengages, lemons (in slices), peaches, pears, raspberries and rhubarb.

Recommended storage time: 12 months for most vegetables, if blanched, and 12 months for most firm fruits; 4 months for soft fruits.

TRICKS OF THE TRADE

Food should look as good as it tastes, and vice versa. Presentation is very much part of the art of cooking, and it is eye appeal which first sets the taste buds working. Some garnishes and decorations are very time-consuming to prepare, but many are both quick and easy. Ideally the garnish or decoration on any dish should be edible, and echo the ingredients in that particular dish. Garnishes and decorations can also help to balance texture and colour; you would use crisp garnishes with smooth, otherwise soft foods, and rich greens or reds to offset cream-coloured sauces. Keep these 'finishing touches' as simple and uncluttered as possible; the food should never look fussy or contrived.

FINISHING TOUCHES

- If a colourful ingredient is used in a dish, keep a little back before cooking to use as a garnish—a ring or two of green or red pepper, a few peas, feathery tops from fresh carrots, celery leaves or fennel
- Leave the small fresh green leaves on cauliflower when cooking it; it looks much more attractive
- Browned flaked almonds add a crunch to cooked white fish, and a pleasing contrast to grilled whole fish, such as trout

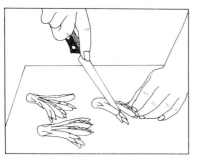

Fanning out asparagus tips

- Use asparagus tips fanned out on top of a cooked chicken breast or lamb cutlet
- Finely snipped crisp bacon adds a pleasing savoury crunch on top of creamed potato
- Sprinkle a mixture of oven-dried breadcrumbs and finely grated lemon rind over cooked green vegetables, such as broccoli
- Give a mimosa garnish to pale vegetables such as cauliflower or Jerusalem artichokes. Chop the whites of hard-boiled eggs finely and sieve the yolks. Sprinkle the white over first of all, and then the sieved yolk
- Black lumpfish roe looks stunning on yellow or cream-coloured dishes, such as egg mayonnaise, or noodles in a cream sauce
- Chop set aspic jelly with a wet knife; use to garnish joints of cold meat or cold fish such as salmon
- If a dish is to be served with a side-serving of mayonnaise or hollandaise sauce; fill a large hollowed out tomato or half a lemon with the chosen sauce

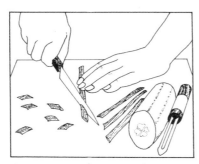

Cutting leaves from cucumber peel

- Cut leaves from cucumber peel to garnish fish mousses and pâtés
- Peel carrots. Using a potato peeler, cut thin spirals of carrot; plunge into a bowl of iced water. Use to garnish portions of pâté and terrines
- Put orange and lemon rind into the liquidiser with granulated sugar; blend until smooth. Use

for sprinkling over the top of fruit pies and crumbles

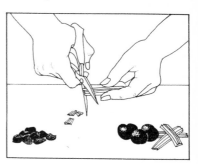

Cutting angelica with dampened scissors

- When using angelica and glacé cherries for decoration, you will obtain a neater finish if you chop both of them with dampened kitchen scissors
- Use mint sprigs for garnishing portions of melon or grapefruit. For a truly sparkling finish, dip the mint sprigs in beaten egg white and then in caster sugar
- A brandy snap filled with a whirl of cream makes a pretty garnish for a fruit mousse or fool
- Try a curl of plain chocolate for a special ice cream or mousse;

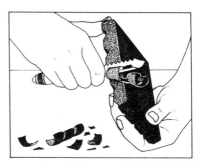

Cutting curls of plain chocolate

use chocolate that is firm but not chilled, and form the curls using a potato peeler
- Sandwich ratafia biscuits together with plain chocolate and leave until set. Use to decorate trifles and large mousses

- Clever doiley-dusting looks most effective on plain sponge cakes. Use icing sugar to dust

Dusting icing sugar over a doiley

over a doiley; and then dust cocoa or chocolate powder over another doiley.

ADD A DASH OF FLAVOUR

- For a strong orange flavour, use frozen concentrated orange rather than freshly squeezed orange juice
- Add an extra piquant flavour to canned soups: a dash of white wine to fish or chicken soups, and a dash of sherry to oxtail and other rich brown soups
- If you are making up a salad which contains quite a sizeable quantity of fruit, use orange juice in the dressing rather than white wine vinegar—it is less harsh
- Use chopped fresh coriander as a garnish for soups which respond to a spicy addition; it is good with carrot, mushroom and Jerusalem artichoke
- For potato salad, pour the prepared dressing over the potatoes while they are still warm—for an unusual flavour add a dash of Pernod
- Cook vegetables in real chicken stock for a really rich flavour

PRESENTATION

Here are some garnishes and decorations which have that extra panache; they are simple to make but ultra effective.

Slicing oranges into cartwheels

Orange or lemon cartwheels

Using a canapé cutter, cut down the length of the lemon or orange, taking strips out of the rind. Cut the fruit into slices. Use to decorate desserts or drinks.

Stuffed cucumber rings

Cut thickish slices of cucumber, and hollow out the centres. Fill with cream cheese, finely chopped red pepper and chopped spring onion. Chill and then cut into thinner slices. An attractive garnish for Parma ham and salami.

CRAFTY TRICKS

- Not enough cream to go round? Fold whisked egg whites into whipped cream.
- If a soup is too salty, add a peeled potato or a good slice of French bread; simmer for a few minutes to allow some of the salt to be absorbed.
- To mend a cracked pastry flan case, brush all over the cracks with beaten egg white. Return to the oven for a few minutes until the egg white has sealed the cracks.
- If you want to make mayonnaise or white sauce to further, thin it with top of the milk, single cream, natural yogurt or soured cream.

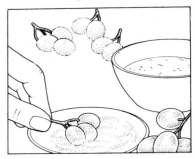

Dipping fruit in frosting mixture

Frosted fruits

They can be used as a most attractive garnish for both sweet and savoury dishes. You simply dip the fruits in a mixture of egg white and icing sugar. Grapes and strawberries look particularly attractive frosted. Use them on platters of cold meat or as a border garnish for elaborate gâteaux.

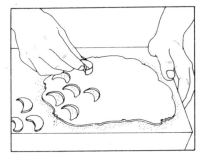

Cutting out pastry crescents

Pastry crescents

Roll out puff pastry trimmings and cut out small crescent shapes. Glaze with beaten egg and bake until golden. Use to garnish fish dishes.

Gherkin fans

Hold the gherkin firmly on a chopping board at one end. Using a small sharp knife cut a series of tongue-shaped slices along the length of the gherkin; do not cut right through the stem end. Fan out each cucumber fan. Use to garnish platters of cold meat and savoury mousses.

QUICK MEALS

With a well-stocked store cupboard, last-minute dishes can be fun to put together, and very satisfying for the cook.

The following ideas are based on store cupboard ingredients, with a few fresh foods as well.

SOUPS

PRAWN AND ASPARAGUS BISQUE
Mix canned asparagus soup with a little white wine; add peeled prawns (frozen or canned). Heat through and swirl in cream.

QUICK VICHYSSOISE
Blend drained canned celery with drained canned new potatoes; add chicken stock and cream to give a smooth soup-like consistency.

STARTERS

MARINATED ARTICHOKES WITH MUSHROOMS
Make a dressing with orange juice, olive oil, chopped mint (fresh or dried) and seasoning. Add drained canned artichoke hearts and button mushrooms and chill. Serve with bread.

MAIN DISHES

MEAT

CHINESE CHICKEN
Cook chicken drumsticks until tender. Add canned sweet and sour sauce and sliced canned water chestnuts. Heat through.

SAUSAGE CASSEROLE
Mix cooked sausages with canned red cabbage, canned red wine sauce, sliced green peppers, dill seeds and seasoning. Heat through in the oven.

FISH

FISHERMAN'S PIE
Mix a can of flaked salmon with a can of mushroom soup and some fried sliced onion; top with made up instant mashed potato mixed with egg yolk and grated cheese. Bake until golden.

SMOKED SALMON FONDUE
Heat canned smoked salmon soup with a little white wine, cream and chopped fresh herbs.

EGG

EGG RISOTTO
Heat ready cooked canned rice in butter with chopped spring onion; add chopped hard-boiled egg, chopped parsley and a little cream and heat through.

PASTA

NOODLE BAKE
Mix cooked green noodles with soured cream, thawed frozen peas, chopped ham, grated Parmesan cheese and seasoning. Place in a gratin dish, sprinkle with extra cheese and bake until golden.

SUPPERS AND SNACKS

CHICKEN AND POTATO GRATIN
Mix canned chicken soup with chopped canned chicken breast and finely chopped red pepper. Put into a gratin dish and top with frozen potato balls. Sprinkle with grated cheese and a few dried breadcrumbs. Bake until golden.

PIZZA-STYLE FRENCH BREAD
Cut lengths of bread and split in half; brush with or dip in oil. Top with drained canned tomatoes, slivers of cheese and/or salami, anchovy fillets and black olives. Brush with oil and bake.

VEGETABLES

Wrap *frozen potato croquettes* in rashers of streaky bacon, and bake until crisp.

Mix thawed and drained *frozen spinach* purée with bottled tartare sauce; heat through in the oven in a covered dish.

Toss blanched almonds in melted butter until lightly golden; add frozen *brussels sprouts*, and heat through.

Lightly cook *button mushrooms* and stir in sufficient canned curry sauce to bind lightly. Delicious with steak and other grilled meats.

PUDDINGS AND DESSERTS

BUTTERED PINEAPPLE PASTRY
Roll out thawed frozen puff pastry to a rectangle; brush with beaten egg white. Top with canned pineapple slices, well drained (or slices of fresh pineapple) and knobs of butter. Scatter with demerara sugar and bake until well puffed and golden. Serve hot with cream.

PEACHES WITH MELBA SAUCE
Use canned whole peaches or skinned fresh ones. Blend raspberry jam with orange juice and a little brandy until smooth. Put peaches into glass dishes and spoon over the sauce.

RASPBERRY ROMANOFF
Crush packet meringues coarsely or, alternatively, use sponge finger biscuits. Mix with lightly whipped cream and well drained canned raspberries. Spoon into stemmed glasses and garnish with a twist of orange.

Sauces and Dressings

These are the essential recipes that are the basis of quick and easy cooking. They provide those vital shortcuts which save precious time in the kitchen without sacrificing flavour or goodness. Here you will find a surprising variety of sauces, pastries and cakes that can be made in next to no time.

BASIC SAUCES AND DRESSINGS

WHITE SAUCE (POURING)

One-stage method

Makes 300 ml ($\frac{1}{2}$ pint)

15 g ($\frac{1}{2}$ oz) butter or margarine

15 g ($\frac{1}{2}$ oz) flour

300 ml ($\frac{1}{2}$ pint) milk

salt and freshly ground pepper

1 Place the butter or margarine, flour and milk in a saucepan. Heat, whisking continuously, until the sauce thickens. Season with salt and pepper.

WHITE SAUCE (COATING)

1 Follow the recipe for Pouring Sauce (above), but use **25 g (1 oz)** each of **butter** and **flour**.

Blender or food processor method

1 Use the ingredients in the same proportions as for Pouring or Coating Sauce (above).

2 Put the butter, flour, milk and seasoning in the machine and blend until smooth.

3 Pour into a saucepan and bring to the boil, stirring, until the sauce thickens.

Roux method

1 Use the ingredients in the same quantities as for Pouring Sauce or Coating Sauce (above).

2 Melt the butter in a saucepan. Add the flour and cook over a low heat, stirring with a wooden spoon, for 2 minutes. Do not allow the mixture (roux) to brown.

3 Remove the pan from the heat and gradually blend in the milk, stirring after each addition to prevent lumps from forming. Bring to the boil slowly and continue to cook, stirring all the time, until the sauce comes to the boil and thickens.

4 Simmer very gently for a further 2–3 minutes. Season with salt and freshly ground pepper.

——————— VARIATIONS ———————

Parsley Sauce
A traditional sauce for bacon, ham and fish dishes.

1 Follow the recipe for the Pouring Sauce or Coating Sauce (above).

2 After seasoning with salt and pepper, stir in **15–30 ml (1–2 tbsp) finely chopped fresh parsley**.

Onion Sauce
For grilled and roast lamb.

1 **Add 1 large onion**, skinned and finely chopped, to the ingredients for Pouring or Coating Sauce (above) and use the roux method.

2 Soften the onion in the butter before adding the flour.

3 Reheat gently before serving.

Cheese Sauce
For fish, poultry, ham, bacon, egg and vegetable dishes.

1 Follow the recipe for Pouring or Coating Sauce (above).

2 Before seasoning with salt and pepper, stir in **50 g (2 oz)** of **finely grated Cheddar cheese** or any other hard cheese, **2.5–5 ml ($\frac{1}{2}$–1 tsp) prepared mustard and a pinch of cayenne pepper.** Cook gently until the cheese melts.

Lemon Sauce
For fish, poultry, egg and veal dishes.

1 Follow the recipe for Pouring or Coating Sauce (page 150).

2 Before seasoning with salt and pepper stir in the **finely grated rind of 1 small lemon and 15 ml (1 tbsp) lemon juice**. Reheat gently before serving.

BASIC VINAIGRETTE

Makes 135 ml (9 tbsp)

90 ml (6 tbsp) olive oil
45 ml (3 tbsp) wine vinegar, cider vinegar or lemon juice
2.5 ml ($\frac{1}{2}$ tsp) sugar
2.5 ml ($\frac{1}{2}$ tsp) wholegrain, Dijon or French mustard
salt and freshly ground pepper

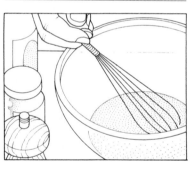

1 Place all the ingredients in a bowl or screw-topped jar and whisk or shake together.

2 Before use, whisk or shake dressing again, as the oil separates out on standing. Taste and adjust seasoning.

Note: If a recipe calls for 150 ml ($\frac{1}{4}$ pint) of dressing, add an extra 15 ml (1 tbsp) oil.

MAYONNAISE MADE IN A BLENDER OR FOOD PROCESSOR

Most blenders and food processors need at least a two-egg quantity in order to ensure that the blades are covered. Remember to have all the ingredients at room temperature.

Makes 300 ml ($\frac{1}{2}$ pint)

2 egg yolks
5 ml (1 tsp) mustard powder or 5 ml (1 tsp) Dijon mustard
5 ml (1 tsp) salt
2.5 ml ($\frac{1}{2}$ tsp) freshly ground pepper
5 ml (1 tsp) sugar (optional)
30 ml (2 tbsp) white wine vinegar lemon juice
about 300 ml ($\frac{1}{2}$ pint) vegetable oil

1 Put the egg yolks, mustard, salt, freshly ground pepper, sugar, if using, and 15 ml (1 tbsp) of the vinegar or lemon juice into the blender goblet or food processor bowl fitted with the metal blade. Blend well together.

2 If your machine has a variable speed control, run it at a slow speed. Add the oil drop by drop through the top of the blender goblet or the feed tube of the processor while the machine is running, until the egg and oil emulsify and become thick. Continue adding the oil gradually in a thin, steady stream. If the mayonnaise becomes too thick, add a little more of the vinegar or of the lemon juice.

3 When all the oil has been added, gradually add the remaining vinegar or lemon juice with the machine still running and blend thoroughly. Taste and adjust seasoning before serving.

STORING MAYONNAISE
Homemade mayonnaise does not keep as long as bought varieties as it is free from added emulsifiers, stabilisers and preservatives. The freshness of the eggs and oil used and the temperature at which it is stored also affect how long it will keep. Mayonnaise keeps for 1 week in the refrigerator in a screw-topped glass jar.

RESCUE REMEDIES
If the mayonnaise separates while you are making it, don't worry there are ways to save it. All these ways involve beating the curdled mixture into a fresh base.

This base can be any one of the following: 5 ml (1 tsp) hot water; 5 ml (1 tsp) vinegar or lemon juice; 5 ml (1 tsp) Dijon mustard or 2.5 ml ($\frac{1}{2}$ tsp) mustard powder (the mayonnaise will taste more strongly of mustard than usual); or a fresh egg yolk to every 300 ml ($\frac{1}{2}$ pint) of mayonnaise. Add the curdled mixture to the base, beating hard. When the mixture is smooth, continue adding the oil as above. (If you use an extra egg yolk you may find that you need to add extra oil.)

───── VARIATIONS ─────

These variations are made by adding the ingredients to 300 ml ($\frac{1}{2}$ pint) mayonnaise.
Caper mayonnaise Add **60 ml (4 tsp) chopped capers, 10 ml (2 tsp) chopped pimento** and **5 ml (1 tsp) tarragon vinegar**. Caper mayonnaise makes an ideal accompaniment for fish.
Celery mayonnaise Add **30 ml (2 tbsp) chopped celery** and **30 ml (2 tbsp) snipped fresh chives.**
Cucumber mayonnaise Add **60 ml (4 tbsp) finely chopped cucumber.** This mayonnaise goes well with fish salads, especially crab, lobster or salmon.
Herb mayonnaise Add **60 ml (4 tbsp) snipped fresh chives** and **30 ml (2 tbsp) chopped fresh parsley.** This mayonnaise goes well with hard-boiled eggs.
Horseradish mayonnaise Add **30 ml (2 tbsp) horseradish sauce.**
Piquant mayonnaise Add **10 ml (2 tsp) tomato ketchup, 10 ml (2 tsp) chopped stuffed olives** and **a pinch of paprika.**

HOLLANDAISE SAUCE MADE IN A BLENDER OR FOOD PROCESSOR

Makes about 150 ml ($\frac{1}{4}$ pint)

2 egg yolks

salt and freshly ground pepper

30 ml (2 tbsp) wine or tarragon vinegar or lemon juice

15 ml (1 tbsp) water

75–100 g (3–4 oz) butter

1 Put the egg yolks and seasoning into the blender goblet or food processor bowl fitted with the metal blade. Blend well together.

2 Put the vinegar or lemon juice and water in a small pan and boil until reduced to about 15 ml (1 tbsp). At the same time, melt the butter in another pan and bring to the boil.

3 With the machine running, add the boiling vinegar then the butter in a slow, steady stream through the top of the machine or through the feeder tube, then mix well.

4 Taste the sauce—if it is too sharp, add a little more butter—it should be slightly piquant, almost thick enough to hold its shape.

5 Turn into a warmed serving jug. Serve warm rather than hot. It is excellent with fish in particular but it is also good with asparagus, broccoli or poached eggs.

——————— VARIATION ———————

Mousseline Sauce
Stir 15–30 ml (1–2 tbsp) whipped double cream into the sauce before serving.

QUICK TOMATO SAUCE

Makes about 450 ml ($\frac{3}{4}$ pint)

397 g (14 oz) can tomatoes

5 ml (1 tsp) tomato purée

1 small onion, skinned and chopped

1 clove garlic, skinned and crushed (optional)

pinch of dried basil

pinch of sugar

freshly ground pepper

15 ml (1 tbsp) vegetable oil

1 Put all the ingredients in a blender or food processor and blend until smooth.

2 Heat in a saucepan for 10–15 minutes until slightly thickened. Serve on pasta or use in made-up dishes.

BARBECUE SAUCE

Makes about 450 ml ($\frac{3}{4}$ pint)

1 medium onion, skinned and chopped or 30 ml (2 tbsp) dried onions

60 ml (4 tbsp) malt vinegar

75 g (3 oz) soft brown sugar

5 ml (1 tsp) mustard powder

30 ml (2 tbsp) Worcestershire sauce

150 ml ($\frac{1}{4}$ pint) tomato ketchup

300 ml ($\frac{1}{2}$ pint) water

salt and freshly ground pepper

5 ml (1 tsp) lemon juice

1 Put all ingredients in a pan. Bring to the boil and simmer gently for 15 minutes, stirring occasionally, until slightly thickened.

2 Strain through a sieve. Heat in a saucepan before serving with sausages, hamburgers or chops.

PIMENTO AND PAPRIKA SAUCE

Makes 450 ml ($\frac{3}{4}$ pint)

40 g ($1\frac{1}{2}$ oz) butter

15 ml (1 tbsp) paprika

45 ml (3 tbsp) flour

450 ml ($\frac{3}{4}$ pint) stock

salt and freshly ground pepper

5 ml (1 tsp) lemon juice

30 ml (2 tbsp) red wine

115 g (4 oz) can pimento, drained and thinly sliced

1 Melt the butter in a saucepan, stir in the paprika and flour and cook gently for 2 minutes.

2 Remove the pan from the heat and gradually stir in the stock, beating well after each addition.

3 Bring to the boil and continue to cook, stirring until the sauce thickens. Simmer for 5 minutes.

4 Season. Add lemon juice, red wine and pimentos. Reheat, and check for seasoning. Serve with cauliflower, celeriac and marrow.

SWEET AND SOUR SAUCE

Makes about 450 ml ($\frac{3}{4}$ pint)

75 g (3 oz) sugar

60 ml (4 tbsp) cider vinegar

45 ml (3 tbsp) soy sauce

30 ml (2 tbsp) cornflour

300 ml ($\frac{1}{2}$ pint) water

1 green pepper, blanched and cut into thin strips

225 g ($\frac{1}{2}$ lb) tomatoes, skinned and quartered

312 g (11 oz) can crushed pineapple

1 Put the sugar, vinegar and soy sauce in a saucepan. Blend the cornflour with the water and add to the pan. Bring to the boil, stirring; simmer gently for 5 minutes. Add the remaining ingredients and simmer for a further 5 minutes.

SATÉ SAUCE (PEANUT SAUCE)

Makes about 450 ml ($\frac{3}{4}$ pint)

100 g (4 oz) crunchy peanut butter
100 g (4 oz) creamed coconut, crumbled
300 ml ($\frac{1}{2}$ pint) boiling water
20 ml (4 tsp) lemon juice
15 ml (1 tbsp) soy sauce
15 ml (1 tbsp) soft brown sugar
2.5–5 ml ($\frac{1}{2}$–1 tsp) chilli powder

1 Put the peanut butter, coconut, water, lemon juice, soy sauce, sugar and chilli powder in a pan and bring slowly to the boil, stirring constantly. Lower the heat and simmer gently for about 5 minutes until the coconut has dissolved and the sauce thickens. Taste and adjust seasoning, to taste.

CHOCOLATE SAUCE

Makes 300 ml ($\frac{1}{2}$ pint)

15 ml (1 tbsp) cornflour
15 ml (1 tbsp) cocoa powder
30 ml (2 tbsp) sugar
300 ml ($\frac{1}{2}$ pint) milk
knob of butter

1 Blend the cornflour, cocoa and the sugar with enough of the milk to give a smooth paste.

2 Heat the remaining milk with the butter until boiling and pour on to the blended mixture, stirring all the time to prevent lumps forming.

3 Return the mixture to the pan and bring to the boil, stirring until it thickens. Cook for a further 1–2 minutes. Serve on steamed or baked sponge puddings.

EGG CUSTARD SAUCE

Curdling can be a problem with egg custards. It occurs if the custard is boiled, so as soon as the mixture coats the back of a wooden spoon it must be removed from the heat. To help prevent curdling, add 2.5 ml ($\frac{1}{2}$ tsp) cornflour to every 300 ml ($\frac{1}{2}$ pint) milk.

Makes 300 ml ($\frac{1}{2}$ pint)

2 eggs
10 ml (2 tsp) caster sugar
300 ml ($\frac{1}{2}$ pint) milk
5 ml (1 tsp) vanilla flavouring (optional)

1 In a bowl, beat the eggs with the sugar and 45 ml (3 tbsp) of the milk. Heat the remaining milk to lukewarm and beat into the eggs.

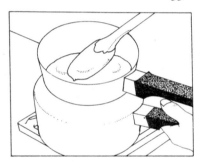

2 Pour into a double saucepan or bowl standing over a pan of simmering water. Cook, stirring continuously, until the custard is thick enough to thinly coat the back of a spoon. Do not boil.

3 Pour into a cold jug and stir in vanilla flavouring, if liked. Serve hot or cold. The sauce thickens slightly on cooling.

BUTTERSCOTCH SAUCE

Makes about 200 ml (8 fl oz)

50 g (2 oz) butter
60 ml (4 tbsp) soft brown sugar
30 ml (2 tbsp) golden syrup
90 ml (6 tbsp) chopped nuts
squeeze of lemon juice (optional)

1 Warm the butter, sugar and syrup in a saucepan until well blended.

2 Boil for 1 minute and stir in the nuts and lemon juice. Serve at once over ice cream.

QUICK APRICOT SAUCE

Makes 200 ml (7 fl oz)

425 g (15 oz) can apricots
10 ml (2 tsp) brandy

1 Drain the apricots, reserving the juice. Put the apricots in a blender or food processor with 60 ml (4 tbsp) of the juice and blend until smooth.

2 Pour the purée into a saucepan and add the brandy. Heat gently for 2–3 minutes. Serve over ice cream.

SABAYON SAUCE

50 g (2 oz) caster sugar
60 ml (4 tbsp) water
2 egg yolks
grated rind of $\frac{1}{2}$ lemon
juice of 1 lemon
30 ml (2 tbsp) rum or sherry
30 ml (2 tbsp) single cream

1 Put the sugar and water in a heavy-based saucepan and heat gently, stirring, until the sugar has dissolved. Bring to the boil and boil for 2–3 minutes.

2 Beat the egg yolks in a basin and slowly pour on the hot syrup, whisking until pale and thick.

3 Add the lemon rind, lemon juice and rum and whisk for a further 2–3 minutes, cool for 30 minutes. Fold in the cream and leave to cool. Chill thoroughly for at least 1 hour.

Pastries

Pastry is useful for both savoury and sweet dishes. The myth that it is difficult to make is soon dispelled with this simple know-how of pastry making. From hand to mixer and processor, all methods are fully explained so you can choose the one that suits you best.

QUICK AND EASY PASTRIES

Shortcrust is perhaps the most versatile and widely used pastry. It is quick and easy to prepare and forms the basis of a wide range of savoury and sweet dishes such as pies, flans and tartlets. When baked, shortcrust pastry should be crisp and at the same time light and firm in texture. To achieve this, you need cool working conditions, cool ingredients and you must handle the pastry, as little as possible. The amount of liquid used in the mixture is also very important—too much produces a tough pastry and too little produces a dry, crumbly pastry which is difficult to handle.

Shortcrust pastry is always made with twice as much flour to fat. Therefore, for 225 g (8 oz) of flour you will need 100 g (4 oz) of fat. The fat can either be butter, block margarine or lard or a mixture.

SHORTCRUST PASTRY—RUBBING-IN METHOD

| 225 g (8 oz) plain flour |
| pinch of salt |
| 50 g (2 oz) butter or block margarine |
| 50 g (2 oz) lard |
| 30–45 ml (2–3 tbsp) chilled water |

1 Mix the flour and salt together in a bowl. Cut the fat into small pieces and add it to the flour.

2 Using both hands, rub the fats lightly into the flour between finger and thumb tips until it resembles fine breadcrumbs.

3 Add the water, sprinkling it evenly over the surface. (Uneven sprinkling may blister the pastry.)

4 Stir it in with a round-bladed knife until the mixture begins to stick together in large lumps.

5 With one hand, collect the dough mixture together to form a ball.

6 Knead lightly for a few seconds only to give a firm, smooth dough.

7 The pastry can be used straightaway, but it is better if it is allowed to 'rest' for about 30 minutes wrapped in foil or cling film in the refrigerator.

8 Sprinkle a very little flour on a working surface and on a rolling pin, not on the pastry, and roll out evenly to about 0.3 cm ($\frac{1}{8}$ inch) thick, in one direction only, turning it occasionally.

Freezing: Both baked and unbaked shortcrust pastry freeze well, although care should be taken when handling frozen baked pastry as it is very fragile. Thaw unbaked dough at room temperature before unwrapping, but rolled out pastry cases may be cooked from frozen.

A 368 g (13 oz) packet of frozen shortcrust pastry is equivalent to a 225 g (8 oz) flour weight.

SHORTCRUST PASTRY—ONE-STAGE METHOD

This quick method for making pastry is completely different from the rubbing-in method for short-crust. Soft tub margarine, water and a little flour are creamed together to form an emulsion, then more flour is mixed in until a dough is formed. One-stage short-crust pastry can be used in any recipe calling for shortcrust pastry. The quantity given here is enough to line a 20.5 cm (8 inch) fluted flan ring.

| 100 g (4 oz) soft tub margarine |
| 175 g (6 oz) plain flour, sifted |
| 15 ml (1 tbsp) chilled water |
| pinch of salt |

1 Place the margarine, 30 ml (2 tbsp) of the flour and the water in a bowl. Cream with a fork for about 30 seconds until well mixed.

2 Mix in the remaining flour with the salt to form a fairly soft dough and knead lightly until smooth.

3 Roll out as for rubbing-in method. When cooking one-stage shortcrust pastry, the usual oven temperature is 190°C (375°F) mark 5.

SHORTCRUST PASTRY—FOOD PROCESSOR METHOD

A food processor will make short-crust pastry very quickly and gives good results. It is most important not to over-process the mixture, as a food processor works in seconds not minutes. For even 'rubbing in', process by operating the burst switch button, if your model has one, in short bursts rather than letting the machine run continuously. Make sure you know the capacity of your food processor and never overload the processor bowl. If making a large quantity of pastry, make it in two batches.

| 225 g (8 oz) plain flour |
| pinch of salt |
| 50 g (2 oz) butter or block margarine |
| 50 g (2 oz) lard |
| about 30 ml (2 tbsp) chilled water |

1 Mix the flour and salt together in the bowl of the food processor. Cut the fat into small pieces and add to the flour. Mix on high speed, until the mixture resembles fine breadcrumbs.

2 Sprinkle the water on the flour and mix until a dough begins to form. Roll out as for rubbing-in method.

SHORTCRUST PASTRY—MIXER METHOD

A mixer will make excellent short-crust pastry in a very short time. As the hands do not touch the pastry, it remains cool, thus improving the end result. However, it is important to remember that the machine works quickly and efficiently, so never let it over-mix or the resulting pastry will be disappointing.

| 225 g (8 oz) plain flour |
| pinch of salt |
| 50 g (2 oz) butter or block margarine |
| 50 g (2 oz) lard |
| about 45 ml (3 tbsp) chilled water |

1 Place the flour and salt in the mixer bowl. Cut the fat into small pieces and add it to the flour.

2 Switch on to minimum speed until the ingredients are incorporated. Gradually increase the mixer speed as the fat breaks up until the mixture resembles fine breadcrumbs.

3 Switch off the mixer and quickly sprinkle the water on top of the mixture. Incorporate this on medium speed and switch off the machine as soon as the mixture forms a compact dough. Roll out as for rubbing-in method.

QUICK FLAKY PASTRY

100 g (4 oz) block margarine
175 g (6 oz) plain flour
pinch of salt
about 30 ml (2 tbsp) chilled water

1 Place the margarine in the freezer and freeze for at least 3 hours until solid.

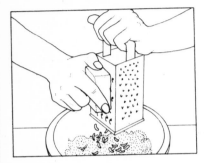

2 Put the flour and salt in a bowl and coarsely grate in the frozen margarine.

3 Add enough chilled water to bind the mixture together.

4 Wrap the pastry in foil or cling film and leave to 'rest' in the refrigerator for about 30 minutes. Roll out as for shortcrust pastry — rubbing-in method.

FLAN PASTRY

100 g (4 oz) plain flour
pinch of salt
75 g (3 oz) butter or block margarine and lard
5 ml (1 tsp) caster sugar
1 egg, beaten

1 Mix the flour and salt together in a bowl. Cut the fat into small pieces and add it to the flour.

2 Rub in the fat until the mixture resembles fine breadcrumbs. Stir in the sugar.

3 Add the egg, stirring with a round-bladed knife until the ingredients begin to stick together in large lumps.

4 With one hand, collect the mixture together and knead lightly for a few seconds to give a firm, smooth dough.

5 Roll out as for shortcrust pastry — rubbing-in method; and use as required. When cooking flan pastry, the usual oven temperature is 200°C (400°F) mark 6.

PÂTE SUCRÉE

100 g (4 oz) plain flour
pinch of salt
50 g (2 oz) caster sugar
50 g (2 oz) butter (at room temperature)
2 egg yolks

1 Sift the flour and salt together on to a working surface, ideally, a marble slab.

2 Make a well in the centre and add the sugar, butter and the egg yolks.

3 Using the fingertips of one hand, pinch and work the sugar, butter and egg yolks together until well blended.

4 Gradually work in all the flour, adding a little water if necessary to bind the mixture together. Knead lightly until smooth.

5 Wrap the pastry in foil or cling film and leave to 'rest' in the refrigerator or a cool place for about 1 hour.

6 Roll the pastry out on a lightly floured surface and use as required. When cooking pâte sucrée, the usual oven temperature is 190°C (375°F) mark 5.

CAKES AND ICINGS

These cake recipes show you just how easy it is to achieve stunning results. Once you've mastered the basic recipes, the variations are endless and soon you will have a whole repertoire of teatime and party treats.

ONE-STAGE FRUIT CAKE

225 g (8 oz) self-raising flour
10 ml (2 tsp) mixed spice
5 ml (1 tsp) baking powder
100 g (4 oz) soft tub margarine
100 g (4 oz) dark soft brown sugar
225 g (8 oz) mixed dried fruit
2 eggs
30 ml (2 tbsp) milk

1 Grease an 18 cm (7 inch) round cake tin and line it with greaseproof paper. Grease the paper.

2 Sift together the flour, spice and baking powder into a large bowl. Add the remaining ingredients, mix well and beat for 2–3 minutes until well blended.

3 Turn the mixture into the prepared tin and bake in the oven at 170°C (325°F) mark 3 for 1¾ hours. Leave the cake in the tin to cool for 1 hour, then turn out onto a wire rack. When the cake is cold, store in an airtight tin for at least a day before cutting.

ONE-STAGE FRUIT CAKE MADE WITH OIL

225 g (8 oz) plain flour
10 ml (2 tsp) baking powder
1.25 ml (¼ tsp) salt
150 g (5 oz) caster sugar
150 ml (¼ pint) vegetable oil
2 eggs
45 ml (3 tbsp) milk
275 g (10 oz) mixed dried fruit
100 g (4 oz) glacé cherries, quartered
50 g (2 oz) chopped mixed peel

1 Grease and line an 18 cm (7 inch) round cake tin and line it with greaseproof paper. Grease the paper.

2 Sift together the flour, baking powder and salt into a large bowl. Stir in the sugar. Add the remaining ingredients, mix well and beat for 2–3 minutes until well blended.

3 Turn the mixture into the prepared tin and bake in the oven at 170°C (325°F) mark 3 for 1 hour. Reduce the oven temperature to 150°C (300°F) mark 2 and bake for a further 1¼–1½ hours.

4 Leave the cake to cool in the tin for 1 hour, then turn onto a wire rack. When the cake is cold, store in an airtight tin for at least 1 day before cutting.

ONE-STAGE SANDWICH CAKE

This is a very quick method of making a cake without rubbing in or creaming the fat first, but you must use a soft tub margarine.

100 g (4 oz) self-raising flour
5 ml (1 tsp) baking powder
100 g (4 oz) soft tub margarine
100 g (4 oz) caster sugar
2 eggs
jam or lemon curd, to fill
caster sugar, to dredge

1 Grease two 18 cm (7 inch) sandwich tins and line the base of each with greaseproof paper. Grease the paper.

2 Sift the flour and baking powder into a large mixing bowl. Add the remaining ingredients, except the filling and dredging sugar, mix well and beat for 2–3 minutes until well blended.

3 Divide the mixture equally between the two prepared tins, smoothing the surface with a palette knife. Bake in the oven at 170°C (325°F) mark 3 for 25–35 minutes until well risen and firm to the touch.

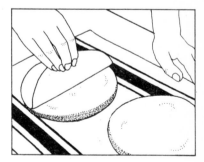

4 Turn the cakes out on to a tea-towel, remove the lining paper, turn on to a wire rack and leave to cool. When cold, sandwich the sponges together with jam or lemon curd and dredge the top with caster sugar.

ONE-STAGE VICTORIA SANDWICH MADE WITH OIL

| 150 g (5 oz) self-raising flour |
| 5 ml (1 tsp) baking powder |
| pinch of salt |
| 125 g (4½ oz) caster sugar |
| 105 ml (7 tbsp) vegetable oil |
| 2 eggs |
| 45 ml (3 tbsp) milk |
| a few drops of vanilla flavouring |
| jam, to fill |
| caster sugar, to dredge |

1 Grease two 18 cm (7 inch) sandwich tins and line the base of each with greaseproof paper. Grease the paper.

2 Sift together the flour, baking powder and salt into a large bowl and stir in the sugar. Add the remaining ingredients, except the jam and dredging sugar, mix well and beat for 2–3 minutes until well blended.

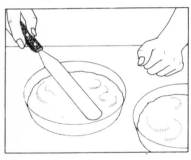

3 Turn the mixture into the prepared tins and bake in the oven at 180°C (350°F) mark 4 for 35–40 minutes until risen, golden brown and firm to the touch.

4 Turn the cakes out onto a tea-towel, remove the lining paper, turn onto a wire rack and leave to cool.

5 When cold, sandwich the sponges together with jam and dredge the top with caster sugar.

ONE-STAGE MARMALADE CAKE

| 100 g (4 oz) self-raising flour |
| 100 g (4 oz) soft tub margarine |
| 100 g (4 oz) caster sugar |
| 2 eggs |
| 15 ml (1 tbsp) hot water |
| 75 ml (5 tbsp) chunky marmalade |
| 100 g (4 oz) icing sugar |

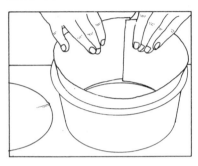

1 Grease a 20.5 cm (8 inch) round cake tin and line with greaseproof paper cut deep enough to make a 2.5 cm (1 inch) collar about the top of the tin. Grease the paper.

2 Sift the flour into a large bowl. Add the margarine, sugar, eggs, hot water and 45 ml (3 tbsp) of the marmalade. Mix well and beat for 2–3 minutes until well blended.

3 Turn the mixture into the prepared tin and bake at 180°C (350°F) mark 4 for 35–40 minutes. Turn out and and leave to cool for 1 hour on a wire rack.

4 Spread with the remaining marmalade. Sift the icing sugar into a bowl and gradually add enough warm water to give a coating consistency. Spread this icing over the top of the cake and leave to set before serving.

WALNUT COFFEE CAKE

| 100 g (4 oz) self-raising flour |
| 5 ml (1 tsp) baking powder |
| 175 g (7 oz) soft tub margarine |
| 100 g (4 oz) caster sugar |
| 2 eggs, size 2 |
| 50 g (2 oz) walnuts, chopped |
| 25 ml (5 tsp) coffee essence |
| 225 g (8 oz) icing sugar |
| 30 ml (2 tbsp) milk |
| walnut halves, to decorate |

1 Grease and line two 18 cm (7 inch) sandwich tins. Sift together the flour and baking powder into a large bowl. Add 100 g (4 oz) of the margarine, the caster sugar, eggs, chopped walnuts and 1 tablespoon of the coffee essence. Mix well and beat for 2–3 minutes until well blended.

2 Turn the mixture into the prepared tins and level the surface. Bake in the oven at 170°C (325°F) mark 3 for 35–40 minutes. Turn the cake out and leave to cool on a wire rack.

3 To make the filling, sift the icing sugar into a bowl, add the remaining margarine, milk and coffee essence and beat thoroughly. Sandwich the cakes together with some of the filling. Use the remainder to cover the top of the cake. Arrange walnut halves in the icing to decorate.

——— VARIATIONS ———

Orange sandwich: Omit the walnuts and coffee essence and add the grated rind and juice of one orange and flavour the filling with the rind and juice of ½ orange.
Mocha sandwich: Replace 25 g (1 oz) flour with 30 ml (2 tbsp) cocoa powder and omit the walnuts. Use the coffee filling.